"Gluten-Free Recipes for the Conscious Cook is a fantastic easy-to-follow cookbook that will open up wo~'' eating pleasure."

—Christiane Northrup, MD, auth
Bodies, Women's Wisdom

"This is an excellent resource for those interesteu in gluten-free cooking. In fact, friends and family members will enjoy the recipes, as well."

—Annemarie Colbin, Ph.D., founder and CEO of the Natural Gourmet Institute in New York City and author of *The Whole Foods Guide to Strong Bones*

"If you think being gluten-free means eating a diet of white rice and starches, think again. Leslie Cerier's innovative recipes show us just how broad, delicious, and healthy this regimen can be. "

—Beth Hillson, founder of Gluten-Free Pantry and food editor for *Living Without* magazine

"With our health and the health of our planet in mind, Cerier has successfully created exquisite culinary sensations using grains, exotic rices, fruits, and vegetables."

—Tina Turbin, contributing writer for the National Foundation for Celiac Awareness, Awareness Magazine, and other publications

"These wonderfully tasty recipes make it so much easier to get the daily requirements of whole grains that are so important to our gluten-free diet. Cerier offers a tantalizing array of main courses, breakfasts, sides, and sweets that are supremely satisfying. Every gluten-free kitchen needs a copy of this book."

—Carol Fenster, president and founder of Savory Palate, Inc., and author of 1,000 *Gluten-Free Recipes*

"In her inimitable style, Cerier presents a wealth of seasonal recipes for the gluten-free cook that are as flexible as they are healthy and delicious. No one will feel deprived with such luscious dishes as hearty greens and tofu in tahini sauce or banana buckwheat pancakes with pecans. Best of all, these recipes aren't only for those with dietary restrictions: a wealth of ideas await anyone who loves fresh produce and whole grains in creative combinations."

—Nava Atlas, author of *Vegan Express* and *Vegan Soups and Hearty Stews for All Seasons*

"The perfect primer for getting acquainted with a wide range of lesser- known whole grains, whether you're following a gluten-free diet or not. The general information on how to cook grains to control texture and taste is invaluable, and the many recipes are creative and original."

—Cynthia Harriman, director of food and nutrition strategies for the Whole Grains Council and its parent organization, Oldways

gluten-free recipes *for the* conscious cook

A SEASONAL, VEGETARIAN COOKBOOK

·{ LESLIE CERIER }·

New Harbinger Publications, Inc.

Publisher's Note

This publication is designed to provide accurate and authoritative information in regard to the subject matter covered. It is sold with the understanding that the publisher is not engaged in rendering psychological, financial, legal, or other professional services. If expert assistance or counseling is needed, the services of a competent professional should be sought.

Distributed in Canada by Raincoast Books

Copyright © 2010 by Leslie Cerier
New Harbinger Publications, Inc.
5674 Shattuck Avenue
Oakland, CA 94609
www.newharbinger.com

Cover design by Amy Shoup
Text design by Michele Waters-Kermes
Acquired by Jess O'Brien
Edited by Jasmine Star

FSC
Mixed Sources
Product group from well-managed
forests and other controlled sources

Cert no. SW-COC-002283
www.fsc.org
© 1996 Forest Stewardship Council

Library of Congress Cataloging-in-Publication Data

Cerier, Leslie.
  Gluten-free recipes for the conscious cook : a seasonal, vegetarian cookbook / Leslie Cerier ; foreword by Kathie Madonna Swift.
      p. cm.
  Includes index.
  ISBN 978-1-57224-737-6
  1. Gluten-free diet--Recipes. 2. Vegetarian cookery. I. Title.
  RM237.86.C395 2010
  641.5'638--dc22
                              2010011983

12   11   10

10   9   8   7   6   5   4   3   2   1

First printing

This book is dedicated to my daughters, Emily and Michelle. May you always cook from your hearts and eat what you love.

contents

contents

acknowledgments

Thanks to my loving family: to my mother, Paula, for encouraging my creativity and supporting me in thinking outside the box; to both of my daughters, Michelle and Emily, for their wisdom and grace and for being such great eaters.

Thanks to Lisa Ekus, my wonderful agent, for connecting me with the folks at New Harbinger. And at New Harbinger, thanks to Jess Beebe and copy editor Jasmine Star for their attention to detail and insightful editing, enabling me to make this book the best it could be; to Jess O'Brien for his positive energy; and to Wendy Millstine for her confidence and support while I was developing this cookbook proposal. Thanks also go to Kathie Swift, for an uplifting foreword; to Dr. Anna Abele, ND, for all the fun we had creating and cooking the Ethiopian Sunshine Stew, Quick Miso Soup with Nettles and Spicy Thai Noodles, Basmati Soup with Indian Spices, Garlicky Peanut Soup, Shiitake Soup with Cashew Cream, and South American Quinoa Stew—all in the name of enhancing the immune system; and to the many students of my cooking classes, who gave me the opportunity to share my love of gluten-free cooking and baking.

Thanks to the farmers all over the world who grow nourishing food using natural and organic methods to sustain us and steward the planet; to the farmers at my local farmer's markets, and to farmer's markets all over the planet, for bringing wholesome and beautiful foods to their communities; and particularly to my CSA, the Brookfield Farm, for providing so many great fruits and vegetables for me to mix and match with whole grains for fabulous seasonal meals all year long. Thanks, too, to the fruits of all of these farmers' efforts: all of the delicious grains and flours I cooked with and ate while creating the tasty recipes for this book. I feel incredibly well nourished. And, ultimately, thanks to the planet, for providing for all of us.

foreword

For over two decades, I have been encouraging gluten-free sabbaticals for my clients suffering from various chronic health conditions such as irritable bowel syndrome, migraines, chronic fatigue, neurological problems, and other ailments. The results have been nothing less than amazing.

Once, I received a call from a client who I had seen because her daughter had been diagnosed with celiac disease. This mom knew that the best way for her daughter to adapt to a gluten-free diet was to have her entire family follow the same plan. So she too changed her diet. A few months later, she called me and explained that for years she had been plagued by a terribly painful bunion and had been to podiatrists, naturopaths, and acupuncturists, but nothing brought relief. Three months after she switched to a gluten-free diet, her bunion disappeared. She wanted to know if I had ever heard of this before. Although I have seen troubling skin conditions improve, hearing return, irritable bowel symptoms resolve, migraine headaches disappear, and depression lift, I had to admit that I had never heard of a disappearing bunion.

Nutritionists and dietitians have known for some time that gluten must be strictly avoided by those with celiac disease, but only recently has research shown that eliminating gluten can help improve autoimmune, inflammatory, gastrointestinal, dermatological, and some neurological conditions. Gluten can even wreak havoc on thyroid function and may be a factor in the twin epidemics of diabetes and obesity. Many parents believe that eliminating gluten is one of the most helpful therapies for children with autism spectrum disorders. I, too, have witnessed dramatic positive behavior changes in both children and adults who have made the transition to a whole-food, gluten-free diet.

But changing your diet isn't always easy, especially when it comes to gluten. Many of the foods that make up the typical diet today also deliver a megadose of gluten. Favorite all-American comfort foods like pizza, macaroni and cheese, cereals, sandwiches, desserts, and snack foods are laden with gluten. Our taste buds have had a long-standing love affair with this substance. I am excited to finally have an excellent cookbook to share with my clients. This book offers truly delicious gluten-free recipes.

But that's not all. Leslie Cerier is part of an environmentally focused movement championing sustainable nutrition and food systems. *Gluten-Free Recipes for the Conscious Cook: A Seasonal Vegetarian Cookbook* dishes up environmentally savvy recipes that are healthy not only for your body, mind, and spirit, but also for our precious planet. Loaded with culinary tips for a sustainable kitchen, this long-overdue cookbook is a mouthwatering adventure into the greening of gluten-free cooking. It will satisfy the most environmentally conscious cook.

I have had the opportunity to teach green and gluten-free workshops with Leslie Cerier in the kitchen at Kripalu Center for Yoga and Health. It is a wild and exciting adventure as she works her culinary magic, sharing her creative genius with each enchanting, earth-friendly recipe that inspires us to cook green and gluten free. I know you will savor each nourishing moment you spend reading and cooking with this book.

—Kathie Madonna Swift, MS, RD, LDN

introduction

Welcome to *Gluten-Free Recipes for the Conscious Cook: A Seasonal, Vegetarian Cookbook*. This cookbook celebrates the earth's bounty and approaches green and gluten-free cooking like a creative sport. I'll confess up front that I don't follow a gluten-free diet myself. I come to this exploration of a wide variety of gluten-free grains as a matter of choice. Over twenty years ago, when I heard that teff, quinoa, and brown rice, to name just a few gluten-free grains, were highly nutritious, I was eager to try them, and I've never looked back. Their flavors and usefulness—not any dietary restrictions—are what keeps me coming back for more.

In these pages you'll find an exciting array of flavorful recipes that will help you embrace a wide variety of gluten-free whole grains and bring them into your kitchen in new and creative ways. Whether you come to this exploration of gluten-free grains out of necessity or just out of interest, you're about to engage in an adventure that will open the door to a whole new realm of cooking—one where your senses come alive with the flavors, colors, textures, and aromas of vibrant and healthful natural foods. If you've been thinking that a gluten-free diet means doing without, think again. There's a world of exciting ingredients to choose from. Embrace the possibilities!

If you're new to gluten-free whole grains, you're in for a treat. In this cookbook, your food choices are multiplied. We'll explore ancient grains and exotic varieties of rice, and I'll show you how to use them in ways you probably never dreamed of—everything from porridges and puddings to pilafs and pasta dishes. These recipes will help you get your day off to a great start with bounteous breakfasts that go way beyond toast (chapter 3). Then, in chapters 4 through 7, you'll find recipes that will nourish and nurture you throughout the day. Just be sure to save some room for a delicious, indulgent, and yet nutritious dessert (chapter 8). So let's get started!

time for a change

In chapter 1, we'll take a quick look at some of the health issues that bring people to a gluten-free diet. For now, let's take a step back and look at the issue from a more philosophical perspective. Everyone can benefit from eating a wider variety of whole grains. In fact, there are some schools of thought that certain forms of wheat intolerance arise from eating too much wheat. Even if eating gluten-free isn't a necessity for you, why not be preemptive and start eating more alternative grains? Plus, all of the different grains come naturally packaged with a unique set of nutrients that help promote health in different ways. Reap all of the benefits you can by consuming a wide variety of grains—and a wide variety of other foods too, for that matter.

And just as exploring the wide world of gluten-free whole grains is good for your body, it's also good for the planet. As we face global warming, we all know that it's time for a big shift. We simply cannot continue with business as usual, including the standard American diet. Adaptability, innovation, and creativity will be key to our success in lessening our carbon footprint, and this is as true of the foods we eat as it is in regard to transportation and or how we get our electricity. By now, many of us understand that eating local, seasonal, and organic foods is essential for our health and vitality, and also essential to maintaining a sustainable way of life—and therefore key in ensuring the well-being of our planet.

So where do gluten-free recipes fit in? In my view, cooking with a wider variety of foods is an important part of the transition we need to make. Grains are a good place to start. For most people, they form the foundation of a healthful diet. And yet there is perhaps less diversity in the grains we consume than in any other major food group. Huge monocultures of wheat and other common grains have damaging impacts on the earth, especially when grown commercially using petroleum-based fertilizers, herbicides, and pesticides. Because many varieties of gluten-free grains are more closely related to their wild cousins than the hybrids we've come to rely on, they can often be grown more easily, using less intensive methods. As a bonus, many of them offer superior nutrition and higher-quality protein than wheat and other common grains. That means more net nutrition from the same amount of land. And best of all, this approach to easing our impact on the planet offers a delicious culinary adventure.

A wide array of whole grains, including many gluten-free varieties, have been worshipped by thriving, creative cultures for centuries. Maize, or corn, was the foundation of early Mesoamerican cultures; rice has long been revered by Asian cultures; the Incas believed quinoa to be sacred; and the list goes on. Pairing sustainably grown gluten-free grains with the local harvest continues this ancient tradition. Let's say yes to abundance!

a few green considerations

No matter what brought you to gluten-free cooking, we all have one thing in common: we depend on our planet for our survival. So it only makes sense to be environmentally savvy about your diet. Whole grains truly are the foundation of a healthful diet—healthful not just for us humans, but also for our planet. You've probably heard about the devastation of rainforests to create grazing land, water pollution from feedlots, and the problems with methane from cattle. And chances are, at some point you've read or heard that eating lower on the food chain is more sustainable, so I'll just offer the reminder that it's far more efficient to eat grain ourselves than to feed it to animals and then use those animals for food. As food resources grow scarce for an ever-increasing human population, it becomes more important to eat less meat, or avoid it altogether. All of that said, I do believe that there's a place for organic eggs and dairy products, especially when the animals that produce them are allowed to range freely and fed a diet that's more natural for them (for dairy cows, that means grass-fed).

Another important way to make your diet more green and earth-friendly is to eat organic whenever you can. For me, it's hard to understand why there's still any question about the benefits of organic everything! Some people dispute that they're superior for health or nutrition. While I disagree, I also wonder about this: Even if these foods aren't better in terms of health or nutrition, they're clearly better for the environment. And we depend on the environment for our very lives, so I'd say that's a pretty huge benefit.

Of course, we can't all afford to buy everything organic, and sometimes there just isn't an organic option. Do the best you can, and focus on the areas where it makes the most difference. As mentioned, eggs and dairy (and any other animal products) should always be organic. Because toxins tend to accumulate increasingly as you move up the food chain, animal foods will have a heavier toxic load. Likewise, it's important to use organic oils because toxins tend to accumulate in fats (in both plants and animals). Some commercial crops are more intensively sprayed and treated than others. You can find lists of these on the Internet to help guide you when purchasing produce. In the absence of a list, think about the qualities of the fruit or vegetable. If it has a thick, tough skin or grows underground, it probably isn't as heavily treated as something leafy, tender, or succulent (bugs just love those!). I think it's especially important to buy organic wine and fair-trade organic coffee and chocolate; this way we celebrate sustainable agriculture all over the world and support the farmers who toil on our behalf while we nurture ourselves and enjoy savory and sweet pleasures. If these purchases ever feel self-indulgent, realize that you're purchasing organic not just for yourself, but for the good of the planet and all of her inhabitants. And if that doesn't sell you on the idea, realize that buying healthful, high-quality food is probably the cheapest health insurance available these days.

You can also increase your green quotient by eating more seasonal, local foods (organic, of course). There's no food fresher or more healthful than what you grow yourself, so grow a garden if you can. It's also good for the soul. Yet we don't all have the time, land, or resources to garden. The good news is, communities around the country are jumping on the local-food bandwagon. Seek out farmer's markets in your area. It's always nice to know exactly where your food came from and to meet the grower face-to-face. Plus, many of these small-scale growers use organic or biodynamic methods. If you aren't sure, ask, and then support the organic growers. (For details on finding a farmer's market near you, see Resources.)

Another good option is community supported agriculture (CSA), which creates a partnership between farmers and local consumers. In CSAs, members of the community invest in a local farm to cover its expenses, and in return they share in the harvest, receiving a weekly assortment of seasonal produce. CSAs may offer other products, beyond just produce—maple syrup, honey, artisanal breads, pasture-raised eggs, cheese, yogurt, and more—often at prices lower than what you'd find in stores. (These may be produced by the CSA, or by other local ventures.) Depending on the climate, some CSAs run all year, whereas others run for about six months. Some deliver to member's homes or centralized pickup spots; in other cases, members pick up their shares at the farm. Some CSAs require members to work shifts on the farm, but many don't. Some have potlucks, planting and harvesting parties, and other events for members to come together to celebrate community and sustainable agriculture.

While local products are always a sound choice for the environment, I think it can make sense to occasionally use imported, fair-trade products from sustainable operations, especially for exceptional and irreplaceable items like olive oil, cacao, maca, goji berries, coconut oil, and specialty rices. This allows us to enjoy the culinary adventure to the fullest while also supporting a global network of sustainable agriculture. This supports well-being around the globe, for both humans and entire ecosystems, and also helps preserve biodiversity.

cooking like an artist

Once you've stocked your kitchen with a bounty of delicious, healthful, and mostly organic foods, it's time to get cooking! Think of yourself as an artist designing a meal, composing with gluten-free whole grains, flours, and pastas complemented by a rainbow of local, seasonal fruits and vegetables. Using a variety of cooking techniques, you can create different textures and an endless assortment of satisfying, flavorful meals. Aim to create a feast for all of your senses, engaging both your intuition and your intellect to experiment with colors, shapes, textures, and aromas. Even the sense of hearing plays a role, and your cooking will benefit when you remember to tune in to the sounds in the kitchen: sizzling, boiling, and even the rhythm of your chopping.

Heighten Your Creativity by Engaging Your Senses

Trust your senses to help you choose and create vital, lively foods. When planning your meals, shopping, and cooking, try to maintain the open and curious attitude of a child. See, smell, taste, and touch everything! When you choose what delights your senses, you'll find that pleasure awaits you. Trust yourself and cook with your inner desires. Your palate—and your entire being—will be awakened, enlivened, and nourished.

Begin by choosing an exciting and abundant variety of local, organic, seasonal fruits, vegetables, and herbs, then select gluten-free grains, pastas, and flours to accompany them. Add modest amounts of beans, soy foods, nuts, seeds, and local, organic free-range eggs and dairy products from grass-fed animals. These foods are your basic palette. Play with their qualities by experimenting with various cooking styles and even cooking times. And don't forget the finishing touches. Most dishes are enhanced by using accents of various spices, oils, and salty seasonings. By mixing and matching all of these foods and cooking techniques, you can create an infinite variety of dishes to keep you nourished all year long. Literally an entire world of cuisines awaits you.

If this approach sounds daunting, there's one more sense you need to engage: your sense of adventure. Have you always been intrigued, if a bit intimidated, by that knobbly celeriac? Go ahead and buy one and give it a try in Roasted Vegetable and Quinoa Casserole (page 70). Interested in reaping the nutritional benefits of goji berries but not sure how to use them? You'll find plenty of ideas in this book, from Power Porridge with Goji Berries (page 46) to Coconut Jasmine Rice with Goji Berries and Shiitakes (page 128). Each time you go to the store, aim to try something you've never used before, whether produce, grains, pastas, flours, or beans. I've given you plenty of recipes using teff, exotic rices, and unusual ingredients like sea vegetables and maca powder. Use these recipes to gain confidence in cooking with unusual foods, and then the sky's the limit.

Balancing flavors is central to cooking. We all have our own flavor preferences and some amount of experience in selecting and combining foods to experience the flavors we love. The recipes in this book will give you many new avenues to explore in your journey through flavors—and the aromas that are part and parcel of the flavor of food. So let's take a look at how to work with the other senses while cooking, in the form of colors, shapes, and textures.

Colors

We humans are highly visual creatures, and the appearance of food has a huge impact on appetite and enticement. Even something as simple as using colorful bowls, platters, and plates adds eye appeal and enhances the appetite. Most grains and pastas have earthy tones that might serve as the backdrop for a dish. Or you could combine grains to create complementary or contrasting patterns. For example, in Bronze Delight (page 119), you can use brown teff to match the kasha, or ivory teff for contrast.

Vegetables, fruits, herbs, and even edible flowers will add color—whether in a wholesale way or as an accent. Brown rice garnished with red radish flowers served in a red bowl is sure to catch your eye. Alternatively, you might scatter minced red chiles and brilliant green cilantro over a serving of quinoa. Or how about black forbidden rice on a bed of glistening, sautéed, dark green leafy vegetables? A simple meal of corn on the cob served side-by-side with multicolored Salsa Salad with Tomatillos and Pinto Beans (page 136) engages the eyes and invites us to eat. Adding chopped red bell peppers and onions to Amaranth and Corn Flatbread (page 141) elevates this humble dish to gorgeous party fare. And be sure to take advantage of all of the interesting colors of vegetables available these days—one of the benefits of growing interest in heirloom varieties and other exotic produce. Colored bell peppers are an obvious choice, and also sweet and tasty. But be sure to branch out with other produce items too. Opt for purple potatoes, golden beets, purple carrots, or striped tomatoes.

Another option for adding color, whether contrasting or complementary, is sauces and garnishes. These sorts of toppings are both decorative and delicious. They can also make a major contribution to the mouthfeel or nutritional profile of a dish. At breakfast, try pouring Blueberry Sauce (page 51) over Coconut Quinoa Waffles with Sorghum Flour (page 58). To add pizzazz to a pilaf, top Coconut Jasmine Rice with Goji Berries and Shiitakes (page 128) with Creamy Cilantro Sauce with Ginger (page 159). For an extravaganza of colors, smother brown rice pasta or quinoa-corn pasta in Tomato Sauce with Cauliflower, Olives, and Capers (page 69) and then garnish with a dollop of Vegan Basil-Walnut Pesto (page 156) or Cilantro Pesto (page 158).

One of the joys of cooking with a variety and abundance of fresh seasonal produce is that the dishes you cook will often have attractive mosaic patterns of colors, as in Millet Apple Raisin Cake (page 184) and African-Spiced Coconut Teff and Red Lentil Stew with Collard Greens and Yams (page 82). Plus, when a meal includes a rainbow of colors, it's more healthful because it's rich in antioxidants and a wide variety of phytonutrients. It's also more likely to include all five tastes: sour, sweet, salty, bitter, and pungent. To me, the easiest way to balance a meal is by color.

Shapes

In addition to being dominated by earth tones, grains tend to be dense. Whether tiny and round, short and fat, long and thin, or almost flat, most whole grains have a fairly homogenous shape. But don't feel confined to using just one grain at a time; you can begin to mix up the shapes by combining different grains. In the breakfast chapter, you'll find a couple of innovative porridge recipes that combine oats and amaranth. Or go wild and use a trio of grains, as in Power Pilaf with Brown Rice, Quinoa, and Wild Rice (page 118). Though also a grain product, pastas offer a world of shapes, from classic elbows to playful spirals to threadlike Asian noodles. And with pastas, you'll find that shape actually has a major impact on the final dish: a chunky sauce calls for a tubular pasta or other shapes that will hold the sauce, whereas long, thin strands of pasta are best with thin, fairly smooth sauces that will coat them evenly. But no one says you can't do it the other way around if you feel like it!

As for fresh fruits and vegetables, for starters take the time to simply appreciate their wonderful shapes. In a finished dish, long spears of asparagus will create one impression, whereas whole cherry tomatoes will create quite another. Fruits and vegetables also provide a great opportunity to experiment with shape. If you're like most people, you may be in a rut in how you cut them. Perhaps you always chop onions. Why not try half-moons, or even entire rings? Sure, it's easier to slice carrots, but if you take the time to julienne them, they can mirror the shape of long noodles or provide contrast and interest to a basic pilaf. Slicing fruits and vegetables in different shapes definitely adds to the fun and aesthetics of any dish. And while you're in the kitchen, also take the time to appreciate how shapes are transformed by cooking: how cubes of winter squash can dissolve into a soup with long, slow simmering; how quinoa grows a little tail when its cooked; how dried fruits become rounded and plump when soaked.

Textures

Though grains may be somewhat limited in terms of color and shape, they more than make up for it when it comes to texture, running the gamut from dense, smooth dishes like polenta to chewy wild rice to crispy granola. In the realm of desserts alone, grains and their flours can be used to create textures ranging from creamy Mocha Coconut Rice Pudding (page 194) to dense, chewy Hazelnut Brownies with Chocolate Chips (page 176) to crispy cookies made with teff flour.

When cooking whole grains, you can influence the final texture in several ways. Chapter 2 will give more details, so for now let's just take a quick look at how it works. The amount of cooking liquid makes a huge difference. For example, if you simmer 1 cup of brown rice with 2 cups of water, the rice will be heavy and chewy. If you cook it in 4 cups of water, it will be creamy and more suitable to a pudding. The more cooking liquid you use, the softer the food becomes. Cooking temperature can also influence texture, as can the way you bring the grain and cooking liquid together. If you add cold cooking liquid to a hot roasted grain and then boil and simmer, it will come out light, sticky, and chewy, with somewhat individual grains. If you add hot cooking liquid to a hot roasted grain and then boil and simmer, it will come out light and nutty flavored, with somewhat individual grains. If you start with grains at room temperature and cold liquid, the cooked grain will be heavy and sticky. (If that seems unappealing, just remember that this is exactly what you want when it comes to oatmeal.) If you sauté uncooked grains before cooking, they'll come out soft, moist, and fairly heavy, with individual grains. And if you presoak grains before cooking them, or cook them in a pressure cooker in a rice crock (more on that in chapter 2), they'll come out very soft, moist, and sticky.

To make any meal more satisfying, be sure to include contrasting textures. You can do that within a single dish. Sometimes a garnish is all you need, as when you top a creamy soup with minced herbs or sliced scallions. Or you can add crunchy nuts or seeds to cooked grains, as in many of the recipes in the side dishes chapter. Jade Rice Pilaf with French Lentils and Toasted Walnuts (page 72) is a great example. Another satisfying combination is crunchy vegetables complementing soft cooked beans and pasta, as in Summer Pasta and Bean Salad (page 67). Another way to bring more textures to a meal is by pairing dishes with different textures. For example, smother a soft grain and bean with a luscious, hot, juicy sauce, as in Red Lentil and Teff Loaf with Red Wine and Porcini Sauce (page 77). And who wouldn't love gooey melted cheese on steamy grains, as in Corn Grits with Sautéed Onions, Kale, and Cheddar (page 81), where chewy dark leafy greens add yet another textural element.

Alright. You've got your creative juices flowing, you're committed to shopping and eating green, and you're excited and intrigued about the world of gluten-free grains. I know you're eager to get cooking, so turn the page and read on. In chapter 1, you'll get to know all of the gluten-free grains. Chapter 2 explains basic methods for cooking each and gives tips on how to expand your grain cookery beyond the basic boil and simmer. Then, the rest of the book takes you on a taste-tempting journey through a wide world of diverse gluten-free dishes. These aren't just recipes for food, they're recipes for a delicious adventure.

Let the adventure begin!

CHAPTER 1

meet the gluten-free grains

Before we get into our exploration of gluten-free grains, it's worthwhile to take a few minutes to understand exactly what gluten is. Gluten is a protein that occurs in wheat and a few other grains. Or, more precisely, gluten is a protein complex comprised of gliadin and glutenin. In traditional bread baking with yeast, kneading helps knit those two proteins into gluten to create a strong, supple dough that's capable of trapping gas bubbles created by the yeast. As a result, the dough expands, or rises. So far, so good. Unfortunately, these proteins also have a downside that you're probably all too familiar with. They can be difficult to digest—or worse. So which grains contain gluten? The short answer is barley, rye, and wheat. A slightly longer list includes cousins or hybrids of those grains: farro, grano, kamut, spelt, and triticale. And which are gluten free? Here's the moment you've been waiting for. Meet the gluten-free grains!

Gluten-Free Grains

- Amaranth

- Buckwheat

- Corn

- Millet

- Oats

- Quinoa

- Rice

- Sorghum

- Teff

- Wild rice

I'll discuss all of the gluten-free grains in detail below, so you can better make their acquaintance. But first, let's take a quick look at a few of the primary reasons people avoid gluten or wheat. The most serious reason is celiac disease. I won't go into the details, but basically, in this disease the body has an immune reaction to gluten that damages the lining of the small intestine, causing a lot of problems and interfering with absorption of nutrients. People with celiac disease can't afford to eat any gluten whatsoever. Wheat allergies can be equally serious if a severe allergic reaction occurs; fortunately, this is pretty rare. Less serious, but still troublesome, is wheat intolerance. This is a vague term, but it generally refers to difficulty in digesting wheat. Folks with this problem may be able to eat a bit of wheat, or they may find they better tolerate sprouted grains or some of wheat's cousins, such as spelt.

exploring gluten-free grains

But enough technical details! If you don't fall into any of the categories described above, there's still a great reason to explore gluten-free grains: expanding your choices and exciting your palate with scrumptious gluten-free whole grains. As hinted at in the introduction, many of them are also eco-friendly choices. As you read the descriptions that follow, you'll notice that many of them are quite hardy and survive in more extreme conditions. This means they can be grown on more marginal croplands, and even when grown conventionally they're typically treated with fewer toxic synthetic pesticides, herbicides, and fertilizers. Plus, many are nutritionally superior to wheat and other more common grains, and several even provide complete protein. This boils down to more net nutrition from every acre of cropland.

In the descriptions that follow, I'll give you the highlights of each grain: history, nutritional benefits, flavor profile, and best uses, including information on other forms, such as flakes, grits, and flours. In chapter 2, I'll provide basic cooking instructions for each grain. And, of course, the rest of the book is devoted to expanding your horizons and giving you a taste of the wide variety of fabulous dishes you can make with these grains. I know you're eager to start cooking, so let's get to it!

Amaranth

Amaranth, a tiny, slightly nutty flavored grain, is an ancient crop dating back thousands of years. The Aztecs believed it held the secret to long life and vitality and celebrated holidays by eating toasted amaranth. Amaranth is actually the seeds of a broad-leaved plant, not a cereal grass, so it isn't technically a grain. However, it works well as a grain and also has a superior nutritional profile. It's a complete protein, has more iron than most grains, and is also a great source of many other minerals.

Whole amaranth is delicious on its own or cooked in combination with other grains in pilafs, and it's one of my favorites in warming morning porridges. You can also sprout amaranth, just as you would alfalfa seeds. In baking, amaranth flour will increase the protein content of baked goods while also lending them a pleasing nutty flavor. It's especially delicious in combination with corn flour, as in the recipe for Amaranth and Corn Flatbread (page 141).

Buckwheat

Breathe a gluten-free sigh of relief. Despite the name "buckwheat," it isn't related to wheat, and in fact, it isn't even technically a grain. It's actually a relative of rhubarb that originated in Siberia. Like other psuedograins, such as amaranth and quinoa, it has a more impressive nutritional profile than true grains, being a complete protein, rich in iron, selenium, and zinc, and a fair source of B vitamins. It's got other advantages that make it a good choice for an eco-conscious kitchen. It cooks very quickly (in just fifteen minutes). And because it's so hardy, it can grow in very harsh conditions, so even commercial varieties are usually grown with few or no chemical fertilizers and pesticides.

Because buckwheat hulls are so hard, they're always removed. The resulting kernels, known as buckwheat groats, are white to pale green and have a mild flavor. You can cook them as is, or even sprout them, but they're a lot tastier when roasted before cooking; in this form, buckwheat groats are known as kasha. You can purchase kasha, but it's beyond simple to make your own. Just toast the buckwheat groats in a dry pan in a 375°F oven for about twenty minutes, and you're good to go. I grew up on kasha in the form of kasha varnishkes, a dish made with sautéed onions and pasta. For an updated, gluten-free version of my mom's winning recipe, see page 133. With its eastern European roots, kasha is a natural in stuffed cabbage rolls. It's also tasty in croquettes, and marinated salads.

Buckwheat's virtues don't stop there. Buckwheat flour makes great pasta, and for anyone on a gluten-free diet (or anyone else, for that matter), 100% buckwheat soba comes to the rescue. Though it hails from Japan, don't feel restricted to using these fabulous noodles in Asian fare. You can also use buckwheat flour in baking. Because it has a strong earthy flavor and creates a very dense, moist texture, it's best used in moderation.

Corn

Corn is unusual in being both a fresh vegetable and a grain. The sweet corn we eat in summer is a relative newcomer that's been bred to retain a maximum of sugar in the kernels as they mature. In the varieties used for corn flour and cornmeal, a lot of the sugar is converted into starch. These varieties come in a range of colors. While yellow is the most common, you can also find white, red, and blue, and the latter two can really enliven your plate with more color. Each has a slightly different nutritional profile, so mix it up and cook with different varieties. (Popcorn is another, distinctly different variety of corn.)

Like amaranth and quinoa, corn has a long history of cultivation in the New World and was venerated as a sacred food. Blue corn plays an especially important role in Hopi Indian culture, where it's used in naming ceremonies and weddings. The Hopis also ate this nutritionally superior variety of corn to prepare for long journeys and strenuous tasks, and indeed it does contain more protein and complex carbohydrates than white corn—as well as an array of valuable phytonutrients. Because all varieties of corn are low in tryptophan and lysine, it isn't a complete protein, but all varieties of corn are a good source of magnesium and thiamin, and a fairly good source of a few other minerals and B vitamins.

For use as a grain, corn comes in several forms: cornmeal in a rainbow of colors, corn flour, corn grits, and possibly popcorn and hominy, depending on how you think about it. Cornmeal comes in many grinds, from course to fine. Corn flour is simply a more finely ground version of cornmeal. Choose cornmeal for more texture and crunch, and use corn flour for a softer, smoother texture. Corn grits are a staple in my kitchen because they cook quickly and are delicious for breakfast, or at any time of day. For a super main dish made with grits, see Corn Grits with Sautéed Onion, Kale, and Cheddar (page 81). They combine nicely with millet and teff, and since all three cook quickly, you can prepare them in the same pot.

Millet

Millet is a catch-all term for several varieties of closely related grains. The type commonly available in the United States is yellow proso millet, a small, round, yellow grain. Though not widely eaten in the United States, millet is one of the earliest known cultivated grains, originating about five thousand years ago in China, where it's still a staple. And because most varieties of millet thrive in hot, dry climates, it's also a staple around the world, especially in Africa and India. Like most grains, it tends to be a little low in lysine, so it isn't a complete protein. It is, however, a great source of magnesium, and a fair source of other minerals and some of the B vitamins.

Millet has a wonderful sweet taste. Because it isn't fussy and cooks so quickly, you can toss it into any soup or stew about twenty minutes before it's ready (this is a great way to thicken a dish that's turned out too thin). When cooked, it sticks together, and once it cools you can slice it, making it a great choice for polenta, croquettes, loaves, and even cakes (check out the Millet Apple Raisin Cake on page 184). Millet is also available as grits, which you can use in all the same ways as corn grits, and flour.

Oats

Oats need no introduction. Thankfully this soothing, comforting grain is gluten-free, but be aware of one important caveat. Oats are often grown in close proximity to wheat and also often processed in the same facilities. For those with wheat intolerance, this shouldn't pose a problem. However, if you have celiac disease, be sure to look for packages labeled gluten-free, which are carefully processed and packaged to avoid cross-contamination.

While oats may seem common, they too were revered in ancient times, in this case by the religions of northern Europe, where they still grow and thrive today. Beyond being a great go-to breakfast in the form of oatmeal, oats are commendable in terms of health benefits. They can help lower cholesterol, reduce blood pressure, and prevent heart disease and cancer. They also enhance immune system function, help stabilize blood sugar, and may even be helpful for insomnia, stress, anxiety, depression, and a variety of other health problems. Why? It may be partially due to the fact that the germ and most of the bran isn't removed during processing, so almost any form of oats, no matter how processed, can be considered a whole grain. Because of this, they're high in fiber, thiamin, and minerals. And perhaps most remarkably, oats have a great amino acid profile and are essentially a complete protein. Why this isn't more widely touted, I have no idea.

If you already eat a lot of quick-cooking oatmeal, that's a start. But I encourage you to broaden your horizons and use whole oats (oat groats) and steel-cut oats, in addition to rolled oats. All make a delicious breakfast cereal, cooked alone or with amaranth, teff, or other quick cooking grains. Because they're bland on their own, add flavor (and nutrition) by throwing in some goji berries, coconut, or whatever dried or fresh fruit you like, and maybe a sprinkling of cinnamon. Of course rolled oats are also traditional in granola (see page 44) and fruit crisps (see pages 192 and 193). Oat flour makes a nice addition to pancakes, cookies, and other baked goods.

Quinoa

Quinoa (pronounced KEEN-wa), the mother grain of the Incas, was domesticated thousands of years ago from its wild cousins in the high Andes. True to its origins, it's extremely hardy, surviving not only in the cold and at high altitudes, but also in hot, dry conditions. Like amaranth and buckwheat, it doesn't come from a cereal grass, so it isn't technically a grain. Quinoa is a species of goosefoot, and true to its name, its leaves are shaped like a goose's foot. Like most of the other psuedograins, quinoa is a great source of protein—one of the best plant sources, in fact—because it contains all of the essential amino acids in a good balance. It's also rich in folic acid and several minerals.

Like corn, quinoa comes in a rainbow of color; tan, red, and black are the most widely available varieties. Each has a slightly different texture and flavor, but generally speaking, quinoa has a light sesame-like flavor. Among its many virtues is that it cooks quickly: just fifteen minutes for whole quinoa. Cooked quinoa is great on its own or mixed with other grains, and it works beautifully in stews and salads. You can also get quinoa flakes and flour. The flour has a nutty, earthy flavor that enhances baked goods while also boosting the protein content. I especially like it in waffles. You can also use it to bind loaves, as in Kasha Loaf with Walnuts and Sunflower Seeds (page 78). And if all of that weren't enough, you can also get quinoa pastas made with a combination of quinoa and corn flour. This truly is a marvelous grain!

Rice

As with oats, no one needs an introduction to rice, which is probably the most common staple food in the modern world. But you may need an introduction to some of the exotic varieties. Not that long ago, the rice selection in the United States was limited to white and brown rice in various forms. Given that literally thousands of types of rice are grown around the world, it's about time we got the chance to broaden our horizons. And what a delicious and exciting world of rice it is, filled with exotic heirloom varieties in a wide array of colors and shapes, each with its own unique texture, flavor, aroma, and nutritional qualities. There's no way I can give you an adequate introduction to all of these varieties, and the truth is, by the time you hold this book in your hands, a few more will probably have come to market. So rather than try to cover all the bases, I'll just describe a few of my favorite varieties, all used in the recipes in this book.

Whole grain rice doesn't have the spectacular nutritional benefits of some of the other grains in this chapter, but it is fairly rich in fiber, niacin, a few other B vitamins, and several minerals. But when it's processed into white rice, almost all of its valuable nutrients are lost, so it offers little beyond starch. To help you explore the exciting world of whole grain rice, I'll give you recipes for using rice in all of the usual ways—from pilaf, salad, and soup to simple preparations that make a great side dish or base for a stir-fry—as well as sensuous, creamy Mocha Coconut Rice Pudding (page 194) and fun and fabulous nori rolls (see chapter 5).

You can also purchase brown rice flour, which has a nutty flavor that's great in muffins, brownies, cookies, and cakes, and you'll find it used in recipes for all of those in this book. For those on a gluten-free diet, rice also comes to the rescue as pasta in the form of numerous types of Asian noodles, as well as a few good brands of rice pasta that you'll find in most natural food stores.

Although we tend to think of rice as a crop that grows in warm, wet conditions, it apparently originated from a wild grass growing in the foothills of the Himalayas perhaps as much as ten thousand years ago. It must have a lot to commend it for because since then it's been bred to survive and thrive in a broad range of conditions, leading to the countless varieties in existence today. Here are descriptions of a few of my favorites as well as some great standbys.

Bhutanese red rice is grown at eight thousand feet in the foothills of the Himalayas, where it's irrigated with mineral-rich glacial meltwater. This short-grain russet-colored rice has a nutty flavor that can bring you back to earth. The first time I tasted it was at a natural food trade show. I was buzzed on organic chocolates and organic wines, and somehow my first bite of this earthy heirloom rice relaxed me and helped me feel grounded and centered. This amazing rice also cooks quickly (in just twenty minutes), which is remarkable for unrefined rice. It's great on its own, or try it in pilafs, puddings, or sushi. We have Lotus Foods to thank for the availability of this heirloom grain, which they rescued from obscurity. If you can't find it locally, you can order it online from Lotus Foods (see Resources). If need be, you can substitute Wehani or short-grain brown rice.

Black forbidden rice is a medium-grained nutty-flavored black rice that has a lovely deep purple hue when cooked. Legend has it that it was once grown solely for the Chinese emperors to ensure their good health, and forbidden for everyone else. In Chinese medicine, black rice is said to be high in qi and to nourish the kidneys, energize spleen function, warm the stomach, brighten the eyes, and stimulate blood circulation. Serve forbidden rice plain to highlight its stunning color, or use it in pilafs, soups, puddings, and stir-fries. It's also great in sushi, but because its grains remain fairly separate when cooked, it's best to combine it with a stickier variety, such as sweet brown rice. It's especially delicious cooked in coconut milk. Lotus Foods is also responsible for resurrecting this ancient grain. If you can't find it locally, you can order it online from Lotus Foods (see Resources). If need be, you can substitute medium-grain brown rice or Bhutanese red rice.

Jade Pearl rice is another gift from the great folks at Lotus Foods. I'll admit up front that this gorgeous, pale-green rice is more refined than most of the rices I use. Pearl in the name refers to the fact that it's pearled, so much of the bran is removed. Jade, of course, refers to the wonderful color—the result of infusing the rice with a bamboo extract. The result? A lovely, soft, aromatic rice that's much higher in fiber than many refined grains, and also loaded with antioxidants from the bamboo extract. Savor it on its own, or try it in sushi and pilafs. If you can't find it locally, you can order it online from Lotus Foods (see Resources). If need be, you can substitute short-grain brown rice, brown basmati, or Madagascar pink rice.

Madagascar pink rice is a russet-colored, medium-grain rice that hails from marshy areas in the Lac Alaotra region of Madagascar. It's grown by a farmers' cooperative and once again we have Lotus Foods to thank for bringing this rare rice to Western markets. It's a great eco-friendly choice, as it requires less water and land to produce high yields, and cooks quickly, as well. It has a soft texture and subtle sweet flavor that makes it ideal for pilafs, stir-fries, sushi, salads, and puddings. If you can't find it locally, you can order it online from Lotus Foods (see Resources). If need be, you can substitute brown basmati or brown jasmine rice.

Brown rice is a pantry staple in green and gluten-free kitchens. Look to long-grain brown rice when you want a light, fluffy texture with individual grains. Short-grain brown rice cooks up dense, moist, and a bit sticky, so it's a better choice for sushi, rice puddings, and rice balls.

Brown basmati rice is an aromatic long-grain brown rice that cooks up light and fluffy. It's a great choice for salads, pilafs, and for cooking in soups.

Brown jasmine rice is an aromatic long-grain brown rice that cooks up moist and tender. Its delicate, almost floral scent pairs nicely with coconut milk and makes it a natural for Asian-inspired dishes.

Sweet brown rice has a slightly sticky texture that makes it perfect for sushi and rice balls. For more visual interest, flavor, and a wider range of nutrients, try cooking it in combination with Bhutanese red rice or forbidden rice.

Sorghum

Sorghum, also known as milo, is a small round grain with the texture of pearled barley. It looks a lot like a large version of millet. In the United States, if most people think of sorghum at all, it's as feed for cattle—or perhaps sorghum syrup. That's a sad fate for a grain that has long been a staple in some parts of Africa, Asia, and India. Fortunately, there's renewed interest in sorghum these days, perhaps because this hardy crop tolerates a wide range of environmental conditions, from arid uplands to moist tropical settings. In recent years, this delicious grain has started to make an appearance in Western markets, so now we can all enjoy cooking with it. While it isn't a nutritional powerhouse compared to other grains, it is a good source of iron, potassium, and fiber, and also provides a few B vitamins. It's even lower in lysine than most grains, so the quality of its protein isn't as good.

Look for sweet white sorghum, both whole and as a flour. It's the best-tasting and most digestible variety. And don't be put off by "white" in the name. That's not white as in refined, it means the grain itself is a pale color. It has a flavor similar to untoasted buckwheat, and a texture that makes it a good stand-in for barley. Try it in marinated salads, pilafs, and soups. Sorghum flour looks a lot like wheat flour and has a pleasant, slightly sweet flavor, so it's a favorite in gluten-free baking.

When baking, you can use a small amount of sorghum flour (15 to 20 percent) to boost the protein content.

Teff

Teff is a tiny grain native to the hills of Ethiopia, where it's used in a wide variety of dishes—most famously the ubiquitous spongy flat-bread known as injera. It's been said that teff was the perfect grain for the seminomadic people of this region because it's so portable; since its grains are so small, just a handful can be used to sow a respectable area. In the 1980s, teff made a remarkable journey to Idaho, thanks to Wayne Carlson. As an American biologist working in the Ethiopian highlands in the early 1970's, he developed a taste for injera. After he returned to the United States, he noticed that the countryside of Idaho's Snake River Plain was remarkably similar to the uplands where teff is grown. He founded the Teff Company, which today grows both brown and ivory teff, and also produces flours from each. Like many other ancient, alternative grains, teff is amazingly hardy and grows in a wide range of conditions, from arid to positively waterlogged.

In all whole grains, nutrients concentrate in the germ and the bran. Because teff is so tiny, the germ and bran make up almost the whole grain, making it impractical to refine, so any form of teff is a whole-grain product, by default. It offers fairly high-quality protein, but like most true grains it is somewhat lacking in lysine. It's high in fiber, iron, and some of the B vitamins and is also a good source of calcium, and other minerals.

Teff's tiny grains have a texture like poppy seeds and a mildly sweet flavor reminiscent of chocolate, hazelnuts, and molasses. (The flavor of ivory teff is milder.) For me, teff was love at first bite. I first tasted it back in 1989 and immediately contacted the Teff Company to see how I could help spread the word. I developed fourteen recipes for them, which are still in use on their website. Two decades later, I'm still in love with this fantastic grain. Whole grain teff cooks quickly (in just fifteen to twenty minutes) and blends well with a wide variety of vegetables, seasonings, other grains, and fresh and dried fruits. In these pages, you'll find it in recipes for porridge, stews, loaves, fritters, and more.

Teff flour is extremely versatile too. It's my first choice when making waffles, pancakes, piecrusts, and cookies, even though I don't have to avoid wheat. As you explore the recipes in this book, you'll find recipes for all of those, and more. Teff flour can be substituted for 100 percent of the whole wheat pastry flour in recipes for pancakes, granola, cookies, and piecrusts; you'll just need to add about 25 percent more liquid.

Wild Rice

Having read about the other gluten-free grains, perhaps you won't be too surprised to learn that wild rice is neither a rice nor a true grain. The long, slender, black "grains" are the seeds of a marsh grass that grows primarily in shallow waters of north-central North America. It has long been sacred to the Ojibwa, who continue to harvest it using traditional methods. Harvesters paddle out in canoes and gently brush the seed heads rising above the water with wooden sticks, threshing the rice into the canoe. All of that said, true wild rice has defied attempts to domesticate it, so most of the wild rice sold in the United States is from hybridized versions grown in rice paddies in Minnesota and California. Support the natives (plants and human) and seek out truly wild rice.

Wild rice is a better source of protein than most true grains, containing a fairly good amount of lysine. It's also high in many minerals and some of the B vitamins. It has a delicious nutty flavor and a pleasantly chewy texture. It blends well with other varieties of rice, making it a natural for pilafs (see pages 118, 125, and 126). Wild rice flour is also available. It has an earthy, nutty flavor that's delicious in pancakes and other baked goods.

---

a few other useful ingredients

So now you've met the gluten-free grains. There are just a few other ingredients that are worth getting to know because of the important role they play in gluten-free baking. While flour is generally made from grains (including the psuedograins described above)—and far too often from wheat—flour can actually be made from virtually any food that you can grind until powdery: almonds, hazelnuts, and chestnuts, not to mention fava beans, garbanzo beans, and even mesquite beans. Here are a few more of my favorite ingredients for gluten-free cooking and baking.

Coconut Flour (and Oil)

Some people used to live in fear of coconut, especially coconut milk and coconut oil, because it's high in saturated fat. As it turns out, its fat is in the form of medium-chain triglycerides. Without getting into the technical details, I'll just say that these fats don't seem to increase cholesterol levels and don't seem to have the same negative impacts on heart health as other saturated fats. Because coconut oil is a saturated fat, it has an important virtue: It's much more stable (at any temperature) than monounsaturated and polyunsaturated fats. I prefer to use extra-virgin coconut oil because it has more coconut flavor and aroma, which I love. I also feel an enhanced sense of health and vitality when I eat it.

But back to flour: Coconut meat can be made into flour, and it too has great health-promoting properties. It's high in fiber and a good source of protein, and also aids digestion, promotes weight loss, regulates blood sugar levels, and protects against diabetes, heart disease, and cancer. When baking, you can replace up to 20 percent of the other flours with coconut flour. Because it's so high in fiber, it absorbs more liquid than other flours. To adjust for this, add an equivalent amount of additional liquid to the recipe. I love it in waffles in combination with other flours like sorghum, corn, teff, or quinoa.

Nut and Seed Meals (and Butters)

For years, quite a few health-conscious Americans had fat phobia and tried to avoid most high-fat foods, including nuts and seeds. Thankfully the pendulum is swinging the other way, and we now recognize that nuts and seeds are a good source of healthy fats. They're also a good source of protein and other nutrients, including antioxidants. In their whole form, nuts and seeds add wonderful texture to all sorts of foods, from pilafs to pancakes and from cookies to crisps.

Nut meals, or nut flours, are another great way to enjoy the fabulous flavors of nuts while also reaping their nutritional benefits. They tend to be heavier than other flours, so if the recipe calls for baking powder or another leavening agent, you may want to increase the amount a bit. Baked goods made with nut meals may be a bit more fragile, but the delicious results more than compensate. You can buy nut meals, but because nuts are high in fat, the meal can go rancid quickly. If you purchase it, store it in the refrigerator or freezer. But the better option is to make your own.

Making nut and seed meals. It's quick and easy to make nut and seed meals. Just grind nuts or seeds in a seed grinder, coffee grinder, blender, or food processor until powdery. There are just a few things to watch out for: If using toasted nuts or seeds, be sure they're cool before you grind them; otherwise you're likely to end up with nut butter (tasty too, but not what you're looking for). And for the same reason, be sure to grind with a series of short pulses. The best nuts and seeds to use in this way are almonds, hazelnuts, sunflower seeds, and walnuts.

Making nut and seed butters. Nut and seed butters definitely have a place in baking. And while peanut butter cookies are always a hit, why not try almond butter, hazelnut butter, or other nut and seed butters? They also make a great addition to soups, stews, and sauces, where they create luscious, creamy textures without a speck of dairy. If you like, toast nuts and seeds before grinding them—about ten minutes in a 350°F oven should do it. Keep a close eye on them and also let your nose be your guide. Whether toasted or raw, just put the nuts or seeds in a food processor and process for a minute or two—or however long it takes. Stop from time to time to scrape down the sides (and to let the motor cool down). If the result isn't as moist and smooth as you'd like, you can add some oil, just a bit at a time. The result may not be quite as smooth as what you can buy in the store, but it will be fresh and delicious, and probably a lot less expensive.

CHAPTER 2

basic grain cookery

Now that you've become acquainted with the fabulous variety of gluten-free grains, it's time to diversify further by learning to cook them in a variety of ways. For starters, be aware that many grains can be used interchangeably in recipes, especially if they cook with the same water-to-grain ratio and have similar textures and cooking times. For example, millet, corn grits, and teff can be substituted for each other, as can many varieties of rice.

When cooking any type of grain, you can influence flavor and texture by using different cookware or different cooking methods. And of course cooking liquid makes a huge difference, and here too you have a wide range of choices. You can cook grains in water, vegetable stock (which adds minerals), juice, or coconut milk (which adds sweetness), or various dairy and nondairy milks (which add protein). Substituting wine, beer, or mirin for some of the water or stock is a tasty option.

To really crank up the creativity and add unique flavor and textural qualities, you can also cook grains with nuts, seeds, sea vegetables, herbs, spices, or a combination of any or all of those. And nothing will enliven your grain cookery more than adding fresh, seasonal vegetables and fruits. Adapting to your local harvest will keep your grain dishes fresh and exciting all year long. Just be aware that swapping fruits and vegetables with the seasons may affect cooking times. For example, summer squash cooks quicker than winter squash. So a sauté of quinoa with mushrooms and summer squash will be ready in just about 20 minutes, whereas baked quinoa with root vegetables and winter squash will take about an hour. That actually works out perfectly. In the colder months, baking will add heat to your home, but in the summertime you'll probably want to focus on dishes that cook more quickly, to keep the house cool.

In this chapter, I'll outline basic cooking methods for all of the gluten-free grains. Then, in the rest of the book, the recipes will explore a variety of ways to mix and match all of the variables discussed above. After you try a variety of recipes, all of these techniques and ideas will become second nature. I bet that in no time at all, you'll be coming up with your own unique creations.

rinsing grains

It's a good idea to rinse millet, whole oats, and all varieties of brown rice prior to cooking. The easiest way is to put the amount you'll be using in a large bowl or the pot you plan to cook in. Add water to cover by 3 to 4 inches and swirl the grains with a chopstick or wooden spoon. Pour off any floating debris, grain hulls, twigs, and so forth, and repeat until the water is clear.

Quinoa is a special case: When harvested, it has a naturally occurring bitter coating, which is just nature's way of keeping the birds away. Although most varieties you'll find in the store generally have this coating removed, to be on the safe side it's best to rinse quinoa before cooking with it. And because it's so tiny, a fine-mesh sieve is the best tool for the job.

Many grains need no rinsing: amaranth, buckwheat groats, corn grits, rolled oats, teff, wild rice, and a wide variety of aromatic rices, including basmati, Bhutanese red, black forbidden, Jade Pearl, jasmine, and Madagascar pink.

the boil-and-simmer method

The boil-and-simmer method is by far the most common method for cooking grains. I hope you'll branch out and try different techniques, but it does make a good starting point because it's so easy. Just combine the grain and water in an appropriate-size saucepan, along with a pinch of salt. Bring to a boil over high heat, then lower the heat, cover, and simmer until all of the water is absorbed. That's it!

This basic method can be used for all grains, but the ratio of grain to liquid varies, as does the simmering time. Consult the following tables for those details for each grain. In all cases, if you'd like the grain to turn out softer, just add a bit more water. Depending on how much you add, you may need to increase the cooking time slightly.

2-to-1 Ratio of Liquid to Grains

Cooking Time	Grain
15 minutes	Buckwheat groats and kasha
15 minutes	Quinoa
	Rice
20 minutes	Bhutanese red
40-50 minutes	brown (long-grain and short-grain)
45-50 minutes	brown basmati
35-45 minutes	brown jasmine
30 minutes	forbidden
20 minutes	Jade Pearl
15-20 minutes	Madagascar pink
40-50 minutes	sweet brown

3-to-1 Ratio of Liquid to Grains

Cooking Time	Grain
20 minutes	Amaranth
10-15 minutes	Corn grits
20-25 minutes	Millet
	Oats
5-7 minutes	rolled (old-fashioned, not quick-cooking or instant)
25-30 minutes	steel-cut
90 minutes	whole (groats)
60 minutes	Sorghum
20 minutes	Teff
50-60 minutes	Wild rice

As you'll see in the recipes at the beginning of chapters 5 and 6, you can also cook several grains together. The simplest way is to choose grains that have a similar liquid-to-grain ratio (more details below) and a similar cooking time; for example, combining quinoa with Bhutanese red rice.

But don't let liquid-to-grain ratio limit you. A bit of simple math is all you need to concoct your own combinations. Let's look at an example from chapter 6, Bronze Delight (page 119). Kasha's ratio is 1 to 2, so 1 cup of kasha needs 2 cups of water; teff's ratio is 1 to 3, so ½ cup of teff needs 1½ cups of water. So to cook them together, you'll use 3½ cups water (2 cups plus 1½ cups).

And there's nothing to say that you can't combine grains with different cooking times, as in Sunny Mountain Rice (page 116). Just be sure to cook for the amount of time required for the longer-cooking variety. The texture of the shorter-cooking variety may be different than if you had cooked it by itself, but that's part of the fun of creating variations!

Whole Grains in a Hurry

If you're like most folks these days, sometimes your intention to eat well is good, but you find yourself short on time for cooking from scratch. I encourage you to make time to cook in a leisurely, relaxed way. The food really will taste better! But I also want to help you cook more healthful foods in whatever time you have available. So here's a list of whole grains arranged by cooking time, for easy reference. This can come in handy for other reasons, too. Maybe it's summertime and you don't want to heat up the kitchen by cooking something that takes a long time. And while I wouldn't want you to make all of your food choices based on cooking time, it is a green consideration.

Cooking Time	Grain
5-7 minutes	Rolled oats (old-fashioned, not quick-cooking or instant)
10-15 minutes	Corn grits
15 minutes	Buckwheat groats and kasha
15 minutes	Quinoa
15-20 minutes	Madagascar pink rice
20 minutes	Bhutanese red rice
20 minutes	Jade Pearl rice
20 minutes	Amaranth
20 minutes	Teff
20-25 minutes	Millet
25-30 minutes	Steel-cut oats
30 minutes	Forbidden rice
35-45 minutes	Brown jasmine rice
40-50 minutes	Brown (long-grain and short-grain) rice
40-50 minutes	Sweet brown rice
45-50 minutes	Brown basmati rice
50-60 minutes	Wild rice
60 minutes	Sorghum
90 minutes	Whole oats (groats)

Cookware

Now that you're clear on the basic method, you may wonder what type of cookware is best for cooking whole grains. Here's the short answer: cast-iron, stainless steel, ceramic, or glass cookware. Let's take a look at why these are best.

Stainless steel cookware is light and versatile. The most important consideration with stainless steel is to use heavy-gauge pots, or at least pots with a heavy bottom. Because they conduct heat more slowly, you're less likely to burn foods when using them. Although they're more expensive, they'll last a lifetime.

Cast-iron griddles, pots, and pans cook slowly and evenly. They also release small amounts of iron into the food, making it more nutritional. I use my cast-iron skillet daily; it is my favorite pan. You can use a cast-iron skillet to cook grains, as long as you have a tight-fitting lid. Cast-iron saucepans are also available; some have an enamel coating. These can be quite expensive, but again, they'll last a lifetime. And the enamel has the benefit of providing more of a nonstick surface without toxic chemicals.

Ceramic cookware is very attractive for cooking and serving. It conducts heat slowly, evenly and keeps foods warm for hours. However, some ceramic cookware produced in foreign countries may contain lead and other toxic chemicals. To be sure ceramic cookware is safe, make sure it's made in the United States or Canada.

Glass cookware is excellent. It retains heat for a long time, and also offers the advantage of allowing you to watch foods cook and bake inside.

A few types of cookware are especially problematic and should be avoided at all costs, especially metal cookware with Teflon and other older nonstick surfaces. When heated, they can release carcinogenic compounds, and because the surface is easily scratched, small bits of the coating can contaminate foods. Because of public concern about this issue, manufacturers are coming up with a bunch of new nonstick surfaces, made of everything from sand to yet more chemicals. None of these new nonstick surfaces have a long track record yet, so I recommend avoiding them for now. (I'll admit that I do make an exception for my waffle iron, as these generally aren't available without a nonstick surface. If you're determined to make waffles and avoid nonstick surfaces, check camping stores for small cast-iron waffle makers.)

Also avoid cookware made from aluminum. On a practical level, aluminum pots and pans are often quite thin, which can cause food to cook unevenly and burn. While you can buy heavy-gauge aluminum cookware, I don't recommend it. Some folks think eating foods cooked in aluminum cookware causes indigestion, constipation, heartburn, gas, and headaches. And although the jury's still out, aluminum exposure may contribute to Alzheimer's disease. And although copper has certain virtues in cookware because it cooks so evenly, copper can be toxic. Stainless steel pots with copper bases are okay, but don't use any pot where copper can come in contact with the food. Sometimes copper pots have a coating to prevent copper from leaching into the food, but the coating can be damaged or abraded, so it's best to avoid these, as well.

Modifications to Change Texture or Enhance Flavor

A few simple modifications to the boil-and-simmer method can make a big difference in texture, flavor, and digestibility.

Toasting grains. *For a fluffy texture, individual grains, and a nutty flavor,* toast grains, either alone or with spices, seeds, nuts, or sea salt, before adding the cooking liquid. First, bring the cooking liquid to a boil. Separately, place the grains in an appropriate-size dry saucepan or skillet with a tight-fitting lid (whatever you'll ultimately cook the dish in), along with spices, seeds, nuts, or salt, as you wish. Cook and stir over medium heat for 3 to 5 minutes, until the grains crackle, pop, or smell fragrant. Lower the heat and pour in the hot cooking liquid. Then cover and simmer for however long the grain usually cooks.

Sautéing grains. *For a moist, tender flavor, individual grains, and a rich flavor,* sauté uncooked grains, either alone or with vegetables, herbs, or spices, before adding the cooking liquid. First, bring the cooking liquid to a boil. Separately, heat some butter, ghee (page 86), sesame oil, extra-virgin olive oil, or extra-virgin coconut oil over medium heat in an appropriate-size saucepan or skillet with a tight-fitting lid (whatever you'll ultimately cook the dish in). Add the grain, along with vegetables

31

Suggested Seasonings

To jazz up cooked grains, include various seasonings or other enhancements when you cook the grains. Here are some suggestions, for each 1 cup of uncooked grains:

- ½ to 1 teaspoon each of toasted mustard, cumin, and coriander seeds for an Indian accent

- 1 tablespoon raw or toasted sesame seeds

- 1 teaspoon of caraway, celery, or dill seeds or a combination of the three

- Other raw or toasted spices, such as a cinnamon stick, curry powder, or a pinch of dried chile flakes

- 1 to 2 bay leaves

- ½ cup sunflower seeds

- ½ cup of presoaked (page 78), raw, or toasted nuts, such as almonds, walnuts, hazelnuts, peanuts, pecans, pistachios, cashews, chestnuts, or pine nuts

- ⅓ cup unsweetened shredded coconut, perhaps with a minced jalapeño pepper (seeded if you prefer)

- A strip of lemon, lime, or orange zest, perhaps with a pinch of dried chile flakes or a slice of ginger

- 1 strip or up to 1 tablespoon of kelp or dulse flakes

- 1 umeboshi plum

- Sautéed aromatic vegetables, such as leeks, onions, shallots, celery, garlic, chile peppers, or ginger

- Colorful vegetables such as carrots, yams, winter squash, or bell peppers

- Seasonal fresh fruits, such as a chopped apple, pear, peach, papaya, nectarine, or berries

- Dried fruit, such as raisins, currants, goji berries or cranberries, or chopped dried apples, apricots, dates, figs, nectarines, papayas, peaches, pears, persimmons, pineapple, or prunes or spices, as you wish. Sauté for 3 to 5 minutes to coat the grain and infuse it with flavor. Lower the heat and pour in the hot cooking liquid. Give the grain a quick stir, then cover and simmer for however long the grain usually cooks.

Soaking grains. *To make grains easier to digest*, soak them in their cooking liquid for at least 6 hours before cooking.

Baking grains. For *soft, slightly sticky grains that split open when cooked*, bake them in a covered baking dish at 350°F, using the same amount of liquid as you would for the boil-and-simmer method. You can toast, sauté, or soak grains before you bake them, if you like. Baking takes slightly longer—usually about 10 minutes, though you may need to increase the cooking time more for longer-cooking grains.

using a rice cooker

An automatic rice cooker is a terrific and almost effortless way to cook rice and other grains. They're highly efficient and make deliciously chewy grains. And, they're an especially good choice for college students and others who don't have access to a full kitchen. Although the exact instructions may vary depending on the model, in most cases all you have to do is put in the ingredients, turn it on, and walk away. Also, you can sauté grains with spices and vegetables in the rice cooking bowl before adding cooking liquid. The ratio of cooking liquid to grain is the same as in the boil-and-simmer method. A rice cooker may take a little longer than the stovetop method.

If you're in the market to buy a rice cooker, I recommend a 12-cup rice model with a stainless steel cooking bowl—not just coated with stainless steel but completely made from stainless steel. I also recommend getting one that has a "keep warm" function and automatically switches to that mode once grain is cooked. Other great features to look for are a glass lid for easy viewing of the contents while they cook, and a stainless steel steaming tray, which is also great for heating tortillas. The best source for these is Lotus Foods (see Resources).

Solar Cookers

Solar cookers are a fabulous eco-friendly choice. They need no fuel and can be used anywhere the sun is shining. Plus, they're inexpensive—or even better, you can build one yourself. In third-world countries, they offer tremendous benefits to people who otherwise must rely on an open fire for cooking, which is often a health hazard for the entire family. For more details or plans, visit the website of Solar Cookers International (www.solarcookers.org) or the Solar Oven Society (www.solarovens.org).

Cooking whole grains in a solar cooker is easy. Simply put the grains, cooking liquid, salt, and whatever other ingredients you like in a pot and place it in the solar cooker. Then just walk away! It's likely to take longer than on the stovetop and the timing may vary depending on your location and the angle of the sun. But no worries, and no need to check them often. They can be left unattended for several hours. They won't burn, and they'll stay moist and delectable.

pressure-cooking

Pressure-cooking is an eco-friendly option, as it usually cooks grains (and other foods) more quickly. Another advantage is that it yields cooked grains that are tender, moist, and usually sweeter. Pressure-cooking isn't as common as it used to be, maybe because people think it's overly involved, or because they got scared off by pressure-cooking horror stories. If either describes you, it's time to rethink. Today's pressure cookers are safe and easy to use.

Pressure-cooking really doesn't make sense for quick-cooking grains, like amaranth, buckwheat, quinoa, and teff, since they cook so fast anyway. Plus, because amaranth and teff are so small, they might clog the pressure vent in some pressure cookers. However, it's a good method for whole oats, sorghum, and many varieties of rice. Just use about ½ cup less water per cup of grain, and decrease the cooking time by about 5 to 10 minutes. In fact, you can often decrease the cooking time even more. Try turning the heat off earlier. As the pressure comes down naturally, grains (and other foods) will continue to cook with the residual heat. As you experiment with this, you'll develop a feel for the timing with different foods.

using a rice crock in a pressure cooker

If you're willing to use a pressure cooker, I encourage you to go one step further and use a rice crock, also known as an Ohsawa pot. (The best source for these is Gold Mine Natural Food Company (see Resources). In this method, the food is cooked in a stoneware casserole, or rice crock, that's placed inside a pressure cooker. I recommend a medium-size rice crock, which fits nicely in a 6-quart pressure cooker. Because no steam is lost in this cooking method, you can use less liquid— about ½ cup less per cup of grain. However, the cooking time is the same as with the boil-and-simmer method.

Using a rice crock has numerous advantages. It gives grains an earthy, sweet flavor that's superior to what you get when boiling and simmering or using a pressure cooker in the standard way. Foods cooked in a rice crock won't burn, and they won't have the metallic flavor that other cookware can impart. Plus, cleanup is quick and easy. Simply empty the water from the pressure cooker, air dry it, and put it away. You can wash the crock by hand or in the dishwasher.

After the grains are cooked, you can keep the crock inside the pressure cooker, surrounded by the hot water, and the grains will stay warm for hours without becoming overcooked. This makes the crock (which is quite attractive) a great way to keep food hot until you serve; it's also a good way to transport a hot dish to a dinner party. In addition, you can use the crock to reheat cooked grains and other dishes. Simply put the crock in the pressure cooker, pour in enough water for it to come halfway up the sides of the crock, and cook at pressure for 5 minutes. And here's a really fun tip: You can make fancy layered dishes in a rice crock, as the surrounding water gently rocks the crock without significantly disturbing the food within. Normal pressure-cooking agitates foods, like a washing machine, mixing them up as it cooks.

Here are detailed instructions for cooking grains in a rice crock in a pressure cooker. Once you get the basic method down, experiment with other dishes.

1. Put the grains, cooking liquid, salt, and whatever other ingredients you like in the rice crock and cover with its lid.

2. Place the crock in the pressure cooker. (Some models have a rope to make it easier to transfer the crock into and out of the pressure cooker.)

3. Pour in enough water for it to come halfway up the sides of the crock. You can use warm water to save cooking time and energy, but don't use boiling water, which could shock the stoneware and crack it.

4. Attach the lid to the pressure cooker, place it over high heat, and bring it up to full pressure.

5. After about 1 minute, lower the heat to maintain low pressure, then cook however long the grain requires.

6. Turn off the heat and wait for the pressure to come down naturally. If you're in a hurry, put the pressure cooker in the sink (transfer it carefully, without tilting or sloshing) and run cold water over it to bring the pressure down quickly.

7. Open the pressure cooker and use a potholder to open the lid of the rice crock. Check that the grain is tender. Sometimes, particularly with millet, the grain may need extra water. If so, add a bit more water, then close the lid. You can probably just let the rice crock sit, as the residual heat should be sufficient to help the grain absorb the extra water. Alternatively, cook at low pressure for another 5 minutes.

CHAPTER 3

bountiful breakfasts

Of all the meals in the standard American diet, breakfast is perhaps the most dominated by grains: cereals, pancakes, baked goods, and, of course, the ever-present toast—almost universally made from wheat flour. I'll be honest. It's rare that I want toast for breakfast. Why would I? There are so many other wonderful whole grain choices: waffles, pancakes, porridges, muffins, granola, and, for those rare times when I don't want grains for breakfast, fruit smoothies, miso soup, or hearty tofu scrambles. If you've been avoiding gluten, you've probably thought you had to live without some of your favorite breakfasts. It's time to wake up and smell the coffee—or just thumb through this chapter. You'll find the alternative recipes I've included to be a real eye-opener.

Beyond being delicious and gluten free, all of the recipes in this chapter will give you energy and rejuvenate your senses. Best of all, most of them are fairly easy to prepare and are very adaptable. These days, so many people need or want to avoid various foods in their diet. It may be that in addition to avoiding gluten, you don't eat dairy products—another major component of the average American breakfast. Don't worry; some of the recipes are vegan, and I've provided a few tips on creating egg- and dairy-free variations. I've even included a recipe for making your own almond milk (page 40).

You'll find a number of recipes for pancakes and waffles—breakfast favorites that you may have thought you had to give up on a gluten-free diet. But let's face it: many people are too busy to cook that kind of breakfast except on weekends. With that in mind, I've started the chapter off with quick breakfasts, like smoothies and porridges, as well as a couple of grab-and-go muffin options. These recipes and their variations may become your go-to breakfasts, but I guarantee you'll look forward to the weekend, when you have time to make Banana Pancakes with Cinnamon (page 52), Berry Good Corn-Quinoa Pancakes (and 54), Teff Waffles (page 59), and other breakfast delights. Pass the maple syrup!

Here's a tip you're bound to love: Some of the recipes in chapter 8, Sweet Indulgences, are chock-full of fruit and use only a moderate amount of healthful sweeteners, so they can serve double duty as breakfast fare. The Lemon Poppy Seed Cake (page 182) makes a great coffee cake. Or try Granny Smith Apple Crumb Pie (page 190) or either of the fruit crisps (pages 192 and 193) topped with yogurt. With recipes like these, who says you can't have dessert for breakfast?

And as for the toast? You could definitely have a Corn Muffin (page 49) or Amaranth and Corn Flatbread (page 141), but I'll let you in on a delicious secret: Fried Dulse (page 172) stands in for toast just fine—and it's also a nutritional powerhouse, packed with a generous amount of protein and a complete range of minerals.

Before you dive into the recipes, here are a few tips that can make the job of cooking easier, and some of them also make your cooking more eco-friendly:

- When you need to measure both a liquid oil and a liquid sweetener, measure the oil first (including melted coconut oil and butter). Then, when you measure sticky liquid sweeteners like honey or maple syrup using the same cup, they'll slide out quickly and cleanly. For the same reason, when making a recipe that calls for both oil and nut butter, it's best to measure the oil first.

- When a recipe calls for melted coconut oil, I find the easiest way to melt it is in a small skillet. Then, if you need to oil a waffle iron, baking sheet, or other pan, you can just clean out the skillet with a pastry brush and use the brush to oil the pan.

- You'll read many recipes that call for mixing wet and dry ingredients separately, then combining them. In my experience this isn't necessary, and it just dirties another dish. Most of the time you can just mix everything together in one bowl.

- In the recipes in this chapter, I've organized ingredients lists so that the information is presented in a uniform way to make things easier for you. But when I'm cooking, I usually add the ingredients in whatever order I like. You should feel free to do the same. One caveat: If you're making a batter that uses egg, whisk the egg first, then add the remaining ingredients.

Almond Milk

When I teach my Great Grains in the Morning cooking class, we make Vanilla Hazelnut Granola (page 44) and fresh almond milk. Before the granola is out of the oven, students have already drunk all of the almond milk. Nut and seed milks are fun and easy to make, and the homemade version are much more delicious than anything you could buy. They're also an excellent alternative to juices and dairy milks. They're lighter and more refreshing, and some say they're less likely to cause congestion. You can use them as the liquid in porridges, baked goods, or waffle and pancake batters, or you can use them in smoothies or drink them straight for a delicious, cool summer beverage. I've provided a recipe for almond milk here; see the sidebar for information on using other nuts and seeds. Many people find that presoaking the almonds makes them easier to digest, but you can skip that step if you like.

MAKES 2 CUPS

½ cup raw almonds
(with skins)

2 cups water

Combine the almonds and 1½ cups of water and soak them overnight or for at least 12 hours.

Drain the almonds, discarding their soaking water, then rinse and drain well.

Put the almonds and the 2 cups of water in a blender. Blend until smooth or until the water looks like milk. Pour the mixture through a fine-mesh sieve, pressing the almond meal with the back of a spoon to get every last drop of almond milk. (You can also strain the milk using cheesecloth or a nut milk bag; be sure to squeeze to get every last drop of milk.) Discard the almond meal.

Stored in an airtight container the refrigerator, almond milk will keep for 4 or 5 days.

Making Other Nut and Seed Milks

Beyond being a great ingredient for all manner of breakfast recipes calling for juice or dairy milks, nut and seed milks are also excellent in creamy vegan sauces and soups, and in cakes, brownies, and other baked goods. Naturally, nut and seed milks taste like the ingredients they're made from. So try your hand at making a wide variety of nut and seed milks, and experiment with using different ones in different recipes. I like almond milk and hazelnut milk over granola and for baking brownies and other pastries because they are light and sweet.

There is a debate about presoaking nuts and seeds before making nut and seed milk. Many avid raw food enthusiast maintain that hazelnuts, Brazil nuts, and hempseeds are the only ones that are so easy to digest that you can forgo presoaking. For all other varieties of nuts and seeds, you might experiment with presoaking and see what your body likes. Use the method for almond milk, adjusting the amount of water as indicated below. When you soak nuts and seeds, they'll swell to approximately double in size. Note that the amount of water referred to in the charts is for the starting, presoaked volume of nuts or seeds. For example, if you soak 1 cup of almonds overnight, you'll have 2 cups of almonds in the morning. However, you'd still use 4 cups of water to make the almond milk.

Per cup of nuts or seeds (volume prior to soaking)	Water
Almonds	4 cups
Brazil nuts	2½
Cashews	3½
Hazelnuts	2½
Hempseeds	3
Sesame seeds	6
Sunflower seeds	6

You can also use this method to make your own coconut milk. For each cup of unsweetened shredded coconut, use two parts liquid. The variations on nut and seed milks are endless: To sweeten, add a bit of maple syrup, honey, molasses, banana, or dates. For flavor, try carob powder, cocoa powder, cacao powder (page 186), or vanilla extract. For a real nutritional boost, add a sprinkle of maca, which will also lend an earthy and mildly nutty flavor. Or, for a thicker, creamier milk with richer flavor, use less liquid.

Banana-Cranberry Smoothie

Smoothies make for a quick and easy start to your day, and the variations are endless. Another plus is that it's so easy to add in nutrient-rich ingredients, like the maca in this recipe. Although it's optional, try to it track down; you may find that a maca boost in the morning helps you get through the day with more stamina and a sense of well-being.

SERVES 3 OR 4

2 cups almond milk (page 40)

3 ripe bananas

1½ cups fresh or frozen cranberries

1 tablespoon maca powder (optional)

Combine all of the ingredients in a blender and blend until smooth. Serve immediately.

Variations

❧ Swap other fresh or frozen berries or seasonal fresh fruits for the cranberries, such as cherries, peaches, or strawberries.

❧ Substitute other nut or seed milks, such as hazelnut milk.

❧ For extra protein and a creamier smoothie, add 1 cup of plain or maple yogurt, which will also give you beneficial probiotics.

Blueberry-Coconut Breakfast Shake

This breakfast shake is so thick and delicious that it reminds me of the malteds I use to get when I was a kid. And between the blueberries, coconut milk, hempseeds, and almond butter, it's a real nutritional powerhouse. You might find, as I do, that a couple of glasses will keep you going for most of the day, or for a great breakfast, have one glass with a Corn Muffin (page 49).

SERVES 2 TO 4

2 cups fresh or frozen blueberries

1 (14-ounce) can coconut milk

5 tablespoons almond butter (see page 24)

¼ cup hempseeds

¼ cup water

3 tablespoons honey or maple syrup

1 teaspoon vanilla extract

Put all of the ingredients in a blender and blend until smooth. Serve immediately.

Variations

For a creamy mousse, refrigerate overnight and eat it with a spoon the next day.

Vanilla Hazelnut Granola

Hazelnuts and cinnamon make this granola taste like a sweet cookie, and the teff adds a subtle hazelnut-chocolate flavor, along with calcium and iron. For an added treat, mix in some dried fruit after the granola has baked, or serve the granola topped with fresh fruit. Although you can serve it with any type of milk or yogurt, homemade almond milk (page 40) complements it nicely; or to enhance the hazelnut flavor, try making some hazelnut milk (see page 41) to accompany it.

SERVES ABOUT 6

3 cups rolled oats

1 cup raw hazelnuts (skins on)

½ cup teff flour

⅓ cup melted extra-virgin coconut oil

½ cup maple syrup

2 tablespoons vanilla extract

½ teaspoon ground cinnamon

Pinch of sea salt

Preheat oven to 325°F. Lightly oil a large baking pan or rimmed baking sheet.

Combine all of the ingredients in a large bowl and mix well. Spread the mixture on the prepared pan in an even layer. Bake for 50 to 60 minutes, stirring occasionally, until the granola is lightly browned. Cool before serving.

Variations

⊰ Use different kinds of nuts, such as almonds, pecans, or a combination.

Teff Porridge with Cinnamon and Dates

You can combine just about any type of dried fruit with teff to make a simple, nourishing, and delicious hot cereal. Here, I've boosted the flavor and nutrition by using coconut milk for part of the cooking liquid. I like to use whole dates here, so there are large pieces of almost melted date in the porridge, but you could chop them if you like. Experiment with different fruits, adding a small handful of whatever dried fruits you like, and feel free to add other spices; ginger or cardamom would also work well. Serve the porridge as is, or top it with yogurt, maple syrup, or any type of milk—dairy or nondairy.

SERVES 3 OR 4	
1 (14-ounce) can coconut milk	Put the coconut milk in a medium saucepan. Pour some of the water into the coconut milk can and swish it around, then pour it into the pan; if needed, repeat with more of the water so you get every last drop of the coconut milk's goodness into the pan. Stir in the teff, dates, cinnamon, and salt, then bring to a boil over medium heat. Lower the heat, cover, and simmer for about 10 minutes, until the teff is tender. Serve immediately.
1¼ cups water	
1 cup teff	
5 pitted dates	
½ teaspoon ground cinnamon	
Pinch of sea salt	

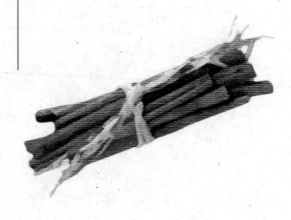

Power Porridge with Goji Berries

This easy porridge will warm you up on a chilly day. The power comes from the amaranth, teff, and goji berries, all superfoods with amazing nutritional profiles. Amaranth has high-quality protein and is also rich in minerals. Teff has plentiful amounts of iron and calcium, while goji berries are a great source of antioxidants and phytonutrients. You can serve this porridge as is, or top it with maple syrup, yogurt, or any type of milk.

SERVES 2

⅔ cup rolled oats

8 pitted dates, chopped

1 tablespoon teff

1 tablespoon amaranth

2 tablespoons goji berries

1 teaspoon ground cinnamon

Pinch of sea salt

2½ cups water

Combine all of the ingredients in a small saucepan over medium heat. Bring to a boil, then lower the heat, cover, and simmer for about 10 minutes, until the amaranth is tender and the porridge begins to thicken. Serve immediately.

Variations

- Instead of a combination of teff and amaranth, use 2 tablespoons of either grain.

- Substitute rice flakes for the rolled oats.

- Replace the dates with about ¼ cup of other dried fruits, such as peaches, cherries, apricots, or figs. You can leave smaller fruits whole, but it's probably best to chop larger fruits.

- Swap unsweetened coconut for the goji berries.

Oat and Amaranth Porridge with Coconut and Raisins

Oatmeal is so good for you, but it lacks pizzazz and can get to be a bit boring if you eat it day after day. Luckily, it's easy to mix it up by adding dried fruit, spices, and various other grains. You can serve this porridge as is, or top it with maple syrup, yogurt, or any type of milk.

SERVES 1 OR 2

⅓ cup rolled oats

3 tablespoons amaranth

3 tablespoons unsweetened shredded coconut

3 tablespoons raisins

½ teaspoon ground cinnamon

Pinch of sea salt

2 cups water

Combine all of the ingredients in a small saucepan over medium heat. Bring to a boil, then lower the heat, cover, and simmer for about 10 minutes, until the amaranth is tender and the porridge begins to thicken. Serve immediately.

Variations

- Substitute teff for the amaranth.
- Substitute rice or quinoa flakes for the rolled oats.
- Replace the raisins, coconut, or both, with other dried fruits, such as peaches, cherries, apricots, or figs.

Oat and Raisin Muffins

Sometimes it's nice to have a grab-and-go breakfast, but if you're on a gluten-free diet, the options may seem limited or nonexistent. Fear not: These muffins are wonderful for breakfast—or for snacking anytime.

MAKES 12 SMALL
MUFFINS

2 cups rolled oats

1 cup teff flour

¼ cup raisins

¼ cup olive oil or melted extra-virgin coconut oil

½ cup maple syrup

½ cup plain yogurt

1 tablespoon arrowroot powder

1 tablespoon baking powder

1½ teaspoons vanilla extract

¾ teaspoon ground cinnamon

¼ teaspoon sea salt

Preheat the oven to 375°F. Oil a muffin tin or line it with muffin liners.

Put all of the ingredients in a large bowl and mix until thoroughly combined. The batter will be thick. Scoop the batter into the prepared muffin tin, filling each cup about two-thirds full.

Bake for about 25 minutes, until a toothpick inserted in the center of a muffin comes out clean.

Vegan Oat and Raisin Muffins: For a vegan muffin, omit the yogurt, add ⅔ cup water, and increase the amount of oil to ½ cup.

Corn Muffins

People of all ages love these delicious muffins, which are equally good with lunch or dinner as they are with breakfast.

MAKES 12 SMALL MUFFINS OR 1 STANDARD LOAF

2 eggs

1 cup apple or pear juice

¼ cup melted unsalted butter

¼ cup maple syrup

1½ teaspoons vanilla extract

1 cup corn flour

1 cup brown rice flour

1½ teaspoons baking powder

½ teaspoon sea salt

Preheat the oven to 350°F. Oil a muffin tin or line it with paper liners, or oil a standard loaf pan.

Whisk the eggs in a large mixing bowl. Stir in the juice, melted butter, maple syrup, and vanilla extract. Add the flours, baking powder, and salt and stir until well combined. Scoop the batter into the prepared muffin tin, filling each cup about two-thirds full, or pour the batter into the loaf pan.

Bake until a toothpick inserted in the center comes out clean (15 to 20 minutes for muffins, or 30 to 40 minutes for a loaf).

Variations

- For a bit more texture, use blue cornmeal or regular cornmeal instead of corn flour; all yield excellent results.

- For added nutrition and flavor, substitute 1 tablespoon of maca powder for 1 tablespoon of the brown rice flour.

Vegan Corn Muffins: Use extra virgin coconut oil or canola oil instead of the butter. Omit the eggs and add 2½ tablespoons of flaxseeds. Grind the flaxseeds in the blender until they're powdery, then add the juice and blend until the mixture is gelatinous. Otherwise, follow directions above.

49

Ginger Apricot Compote

Homemade compotes are easy to prepare and make a great topping for pancakes or waffles. You can use any type of dried fruit or a combination. You may need to adjust the amount of water or cooking time depending on the type of fruit you use and how dry it is. The goal is to cook the fruit until it's plump and tender.

MAKES ABOUT 1½
CUPS; SERVES 3 OR
4 OVER PANCAKES
OR WAFFLES

————

1 cup dried
apricots, chopped

1 cup water

½ cup pear juice

2 tablespoons
grated fresh ginger

1 tablespoon
maple syrup

Pinch of sea salt

1 tablespoon
arrowroot or kudzu
powder

1 tablespoon cold
water

Put the apricots, 1 cup water, juice, ginger, maple syrup, and salt in a small saucepan over medium-high heat. Bring to a boil, then lower the heat and simmer, stirring occasionally, for about 10 minutes, until the apricots are plump and tender. (If the apricots are especially dry, you may need to add more water or extend the cooking time.)

Dissolve the arrowroot powder in the 1 tablespoon cold water. Stir the slurry into the apricots and continue to simmer, stirring occasionally, for about 2 minutes, until thick. Taste and add more maple syrup or ginger if you like.

Blueberry Sauce

If you're lucky to live where berries grow well, I recommend you eat lots of fresh berries all summer long, and be sure to freeze a lot more for the winter months, when their bright flavors will bring a taste of sunshine to cold, dark days. That way you can enjoy this quick, easy sauce, which is a favorite on pancakes and waffles, year-round. Feel free to substitute raspberries, blackberries or strawberries for the blueberries in this delicious sauce, and no matter what type of berries you use, either fresh or frozen is fine.

MAKES ABOUT 2¼ CUPS; SERVES 3 OR 4 OVER PANCAKES OR WAFFLES

---

4 cups fresh or frozen blueberries

2 tablespoons maple sugar or maple syrup

1 tablespoon arrowroot or kudzu powder

1 tablespoon cold water

Put the blueberries and maple sugar in a medium saucepan over medium heat. Once they start to steam and bubble a bit, lower the heat, cover, and simmer until the berries are soft and juicy (about 5 minutes for fresh berries or 10 minutes for frozen).

Dissolve the arrowroot powder in the water, then stir the slurry into the berries. Simmer for a minute or two longer, until the sauce thickens. Taste and add more sweetener if you like.

Banana Pancakes with Cinnamon

Good morning pancakes! You may be amazed (and you will definitely be delighted) to learn that teff flour can stand in for all of the wheat flour in pancakes. Use just a couple of tablespoons of this batter to make small pancakes that are fun to eat with your hands like a muffin. Because they're cooked in coconut oil, they're so tasty that you may not even want any toppings.

SERVES 4 TO 6

2 tablespoons flaxseeds

4 eggs

2 ripe bananas

1 cup apple juice

1 tablespoon vanilla extract

1 tablespoon honey or maple syrup

1 teaspoon ground cinnamon

2 cups teff flour

2 teaspoons baking powder

½ teaspoon sea salt

Extra-virgin coconut oil, for frying

Grind the flaxseeds in a blender until powdery. Add the eggs, bananas, juice, vanilla, honey, and cinnamon and blend until smooth.

Put the flour, baking powder, and salt in a large bowl. Pour in the banana mixture and stir until well combined.

Heat some coconut oil in a heavy skillet or griddle over medium heat and brush it over the surface when it melts. Ladle the batter onto the hot pan to make 3-inch pancakes. Cook for about 1½ minutes, until the tops are bubbly and the edges are dry. Turn the pancakes over and cook for about 1 more minute, until the bottoms are brown. Serve immediately.

Variations

❧ Swap other juices, such as peach or pear, for the apple juice.

❧ Substitute any dairy or nondairy milk for the juice.

Banana Buckwheat Pancakes with Pecans

In these sweet and filling vegan pancakes, bananas bind the batter like eggs would. And in combination with the pecans, the bananas also balance the bold flavor of the buckwheat flour. Since buckwheat is a complete protein, these pancakes are a great way to start your day, especially when topped with Ginger Apricot Compote (page 50).

SERVES 4 TO 6

3 bananas

1½ cups apple or pear juice

3 tablespoons maple syrup

1½ teaspoons vanilla

1½ cups buckwheat flour

6 tablespoons chopped raw pecans

2 teaspoons baking powder

½ teaspoon sea salt

Extra-virgin coconut oil for frying

Put the bananas, juice, maple syrup and vanilla in a blender and blend until smooth.

Put the flour, pecans, baking powder, and salt in a large bowl. Pour in the banana mixture and stir until well combined.

Heat some coconut oil in a heavy skillet or griddle over medium heat and brush it over the surface when it melts. Ladle the batter onto the hot pan to make 3-inch pancakes. Cook for about 1½ minutes, until the tops are bubbly and the edges are dry. Turn the pancakes over and cook for about 1 more minute, until the bottoms are brown. Serve immediately.

Berry Good Corn-Quinoa Pancakes

The combination of fresh blueberries and strawberry nectar gives these pancakes a great flavor and an impressive array of phytonutrients. That said, you could use almost any fruit juice or dairy or nut milk in this recipe. Experiment with different flours, too. You could use all teff flour or a different combination of gluten-free flours. The one thing to watch out for is coconut flour. It absorbs more liquid, so if you add more than about a tablespoon of coconut flour, you'd need to add more liquid.

SERVES 4 TO 6

4 eggs

1 cup strawberry nectar

½ cup melted extra-virgin coconut oil

½ cup maple syrup

4 teaspoons vanilla extract

1 cup corn flour

1 cup quinoa flour

1 tablespoon baking powder

½ teaspoons sea salt

2 cups fresh or frozen blueberries

Whisk the eggs in a large mixing bowl. Stir in the strawberry nectar, oil, maple syrup, and vanilla. Add the flours, baking powder, and salt and stir until well combined. Gently fold in the blueberries.

Heat some coconut oil in a heavy skillet or griddle over medium heat and brush it over the surface when it melts. Ladle the batter onto the hot pan to make 3-inch pancakes. Cook for about 1½ minutes, until the tops are bubbly and the edges are dry. Turn the pancakes over and cook for about 1 more minute, until the bottoms are brown. Serve immediately.

Variations

- Blueberries not in season? No problem! Cut up strawberries or swap other berries for the blueberries.

- Swap 2 cups of teff flour for the corn and quinoa flours.

- Use other juices, such as peach, pear, or apple juice.

- Swap any type of dairy or nondairy milk for the juice.

Strawberry Pancakes

Full of strawberries, these pancakes are yummy just on their own. Or for a change of pace, try topping them with yogurt. And there's no reason not to enjoy them like strawberry shortcake, topped with fresh whipped cream and perhaps a few more sliced strawberries.

SERVES 4 TO 6

4 eggs

1 cup apple juice

½ cup honey or maple syrup

4 teaspoons vanilla extract

2 cups teff flour

1 tablespoon baking powder

½ teaspoon sea salt

2 cups sliced strawberries

Extra-virgin coconut oil, for frying

Whisk the eggs in a large bowl. Stir in the juice, honey, and vanilla. Add the flour, baking powder, and salt and stir until well combined. Gently fold in the strawberries.

Heat some coconut oil in a heavy skillet or griddle over medium heat and brush it over the surface when it melts. Ladle the batter onto the hot pan to make pancakes of whatever size you like. Cook for about 1½ minutes, until the tops are bubbly and the edges are dry. Turn the pancakes over and cook for about 1 more minute, until the bottoms are golden brown. Serve immediately.

Teff Pancakes with Goji Berries and Maca

For a real power breakfast, try these sweet, nutrient-rich pancakes, replete with superfoods. Coconut, maca, goji berries, and teff will give you a boost and get your day off to a great start. For a sweeter variation, use a little more teff flour and less maca.

SERVES 4 TO 6

4 eggs

2 cups apple juice

¼ cup honey or maple syrup

¼ cup vanilla extract

1¾ cups teff flour

⅓ cup dried goji berries

¼ cup maca powder

1 tablespoon baking powder

½ teaspoon sea salt

Extra-virgin coconut oil, for frying

Whisk the eggs in a medium-size bowl. Stir in the juice, honey, and vanilla. Add the flour, goji berries, maca powder, baking powder, and salt and stir until well combined.

Heat some coconut oil in a heavy skillet or griddle over medium heat and brush it over the surface when it melts. Ladle the batter onto the hot pan to make pancakes of whatever size you like. Cook for about 2 minutes, until the tops are bubbly and the edges are dry. Turn the pancakes over and cook for about 1 more minute, until the bottoms are golden brown (if using ivory teff flour) or brown (if using brown teff flour). Serve immediately.

Variations

◆ Swap dried cranberries, raisins, or other dried fruits for the goji berries.

◆ Replace the maca powder with another ¼ cup teff flour, or ¼ cup of any gluten-free flour. (If you use coconut flour, you may need to add a bit more liquid.)

Blueberry-Corn Pancakes with Maca

Blueberries and cornmeal are always a winning combination. Here I've further enhanced their flavor by adding maca powder, which lends a sophisticated, slightly nutty flavor and boosts the nutrient content. As always, butter and maple syrup would be delicious toppings for these pancakes, but they're also great with applesauce or yogurt.

SERVES 4 TO 6

4 eggs

1 cup pear or peach juice

½ cup maple syrup

4 teaspoons vanilla extract

1⅓ cup cornmeal or corn flour

½ cup quinoa flour

¼ cup maca powder

1 tablespoon baking powder

½ teaspoon sea salt

2 cups blueberries

Extra-virgin coconut oil, for frying

Whisk the eggs in a small bowl. Stir in the juice, maple syrup, and vanilla. Add the cornmeal, quinoa flour, maca powder, baking powder, and salt and stir until well combined. Gently fold in the blueberries.

Heat some coconut oil in a heavy skillet or griddle over medium heat and brush it over the surface when it melts. Ladle the batter onto the hot pan to make pancakes of whatever size you like. Cook for about 1½ minutes, until the tops are bubbly and the edges are dry. Turn the pancakes over and cook for about 1 more minute, until the bottoms are golden brown. Serve immediately.

Variations

⚜ Swap ½ cup sorghum flour for the quinoa flour.

⚜ Use ¼ cup quinoa, sorghum, or corn flour in place of the maca powder.

⚜ Substitute 2 cups of teff flour for the cornmeal, quinoa flour, and maca powder.

⚜ Substitute raspberries, blackberries, or strawberries for the blueberries.

Coconut Quinoa Waffles with Sorghum Flour

There are so many great flours to choose from when making gluten-free waffles. In this version, quinoa, coconut, and sorghum flours combine to create a waffle that's got lots of protein and fiber and is so tasty that you may not even want a topping. Don't be put off by the ingredient "white sorghum flour." It isn't white in the sense of being refined; it's just made from white sorghum.

SERVES ABOUT 4

4 eggs

3 cups pear juice

½ cup melted extra-virgin coconut oil or butter

¼ cup maple syrup or honey

¼ cup vanilla extract

1 cup quinoa flour

½ cup coconut flour

½ cup white sorghum flour

1 tablespoon baking powder

½ teaspoon sea salt

Preheat the waffle iron.

Whisk the eggs in a medium-size bowl. Stir in the juice, oil, maple syrup, and vanilla. Add the flours, baking powder, and salt and stir until well combined.

Brush both the top and bottom surface of the waffle iron with oil, then ladle in enough batter to almost cover the bottom surface of the iron. Cook until the steaming stops or the waffle is golden brown. Serve immediately, or keep the cooked waffles in a warm oven until you're ready to serve (see page 60).

Variations

❧ Use 2 cups teff flour in place of the quinoa, coconut, and sorghum flour.

❧ Swap other juices, such as peach or apple juice.

❧ Swap soy, rice, almond, hazelnut, cow, or goat milk for juice.

Teff Waffles

These waffles are like having a little cake for breakfast and are delicious with or without a topping. There's enough maple syrup in the batter that I never feel a need to pour more on top; I just eat them out of hand, like a muffin. If you make these in autumn, try using fresh apple cider for a real treat.

SERVES 3

4 eggs

¾ cup apple juice or apple cider

3 tablespoons melted extra-virgin coconut oil or butter

3 tablespoons maple syrup

1 tablespoon vanilla extract

1½ cups teff flour

1 tablespoon baking powder

½ teaspoon sea salt

Preheat the waffle iron.

Whisk the eggs in a large bowl. Stir in the juice, oil, maple syrup, and vanilla. Add the flour, baking powder, and salt and stir until well combined.

Brush both the top and bottom surface of the waffle iron with oil, then ladle in enough batter to cover the bottom surface of the iron. Cook until the steaming stops or the waffle is golden brown. Serve immediately, or keep the cooked waffles in a warm oven until you're ready to serve (see page 60).

Variations

⋙ For a sophisticated variation, use 1⅓ cups of teff flour plus 2 tablespoons maca powder.

59

Hints and Tips for Waffle Making

When it comes to making waffles, my first tip—and probably the most important—is to practice. It's hard to give precise instructions in recipes for a lot of reasons. For starters, different models of waffle makers take different amounts of batter, and they tend to cook differently, too. (For details, read the instructions that came with your waffle maker. If you don't have them, don't worry; a quick Internet search will usually turn up some documentation.) Sometimes it seems like each waffle iron has its own personality, so get to know yours on a personal basis. This is where practice comes in. If you use your waffle iron frequently, you'll soon be making perfect waffles every time. Here are some specific hints and tips:

- Any pancake batter can be used as a waffle batter, and vice versa. For pancakes, simply omit the oil. If converting pancake batter to make waffles, add about 2 tablespoons of oil per cup of flour in the recipe. (Add more oil if there is fresh or dried fruit in the batter and for richer, lighter, and possibly more crispy waffles.) As you get more experience in making both, you'll develop a feel for how thick the batter should be to make pancakes or waffles to your liking.

- As a rough guideline, for each ½ cup of flour in the batter, count on about one serving.

- As mentioned, different models of waffle irons take different amounts of batter. The amount may also vary depending on the thickness of the batter. You'll need less of a thin batter and more of a thick batter, and you may have to use a spoon or spatula to help spread a thicker batter. In any case, try to avoid adding so much batter that it comes within about 1 inch of the edge. When you close the top, the batter will spread a bit.

- Waffles generally take about 4 minutes to cook. If you try to open the lid and it resists, wait a moment longer; this generally means that the waffle isn't finished cooking yet.

- It may sound self-indulgent, but why not make waffles for just one person? Go ahead and spoil yourself. You're worth it! In fact, I prefer making waffles for just me, rather than a group, since you can only make one at a time.

- Sticking is probably the must frustrating aspect of cooking waffles. Sadly, what starts as a nonstick coating has a tendency to become non-nonstick over time... No matter how old (or new) your waffle maker, avoid problems by always brushing both the bottom and top surfaces with a generous amount of oil. (It's best to do the bottom surface first, as the oil you brush on the top surface will start sliding down and dripping almost immediately.)

- Be especially generous with the oil if you'll be including fresh fruit in your waffle batter; it has a tendency to stick.

- I recommend brushing the waffle iron with extra-virgin coconut oil to impart a delicious coconut flavor.

- To clean a waffle iron, wipe it down with a soft towel. In the unfortunate event that you do get some sticking, let the waffle iron cool, then simply brush the crumbs off with a soft, dry brush.

- If you're making multiple waffles and would like to serve them all at once, put finished waffles in a single layer on a baking sheet in warm oven (about 200°F) until you've finished cooking all of them. (After you make the first waffle, let the waffle iron heat up again, then brush with oil as needed before cooking another.)

- My gluten-free pancake and waffle recipes are very forgiving and allow for slight variations. Have fun and follow the recipes as they are, and then feel free to use the variations as a springboard for creating your own versions!

Corn and Quinoa Waffles with Maca

Maca powder, made from the root of an herbaceous plant, has been revered by Andean cultures for centuries, if not millennia, for both its delicious earthy, nutty flavor and its healthful properties. It's packed with vitamins and minerals and said to increase stamina and libido. Because its flavor is strong, a little goes a long way.

SERVES 2 OR 3

3 eggs

⅔ cup peach juice

2 tablespoons melted butter or extra-virgin coconut oil

2 tablespoons maple syrup or honey

1 teaspoon vanilla extract

1 teaspoon almond extract

½ cup corn flour

½ cup quinoa flour

1 tablespoon maca powder

2 teaspoons baking powder

½ teaspoon sea salt

Preheat the waffle iron.

Whisk the eggs in a medium-size bowl. Stir in the juice, melted butter, maple syrup, and extracts. Add the flours, maca powder, baking powder, and salt and stir until well combined.

Brush both the top and bottom surfaces of the waffle iron with oil, then ladle in enough batter to almost cover the bottom surface of the iron. Cook until the steaming stops or the waffle is golden brown. Serve immediately, or keep the cooked waffles in a warm oven until you're ready to serve (see page 60).

Variations

- For a bit more texture, use blue cornmeal or regular cornmeal instead of corn flour; all yield excellent (and delicious!) results.

- Use another tablespoon of corn flour or quinoa flour in place of the maca powder.

- Swap other juices, such as apple juice, for the peach juice.

- Swap any type of dairy or nondairy milk for the juice.

Scrambled Tofu with Sweet Corn and Collard Greens

Fresh corn is the sweetest the day it's picked. However, for convenience I often steam more than I can eat so I can snack on it and add it to dishes the next day. Here it's combined with other seasonal vegetables and tofu for a hearty late summer breakfast treat. Tumeric lends the tofu an appealing golden color. Nutritional yeast gives a rich, almost cheesy flavor, and is also a great source of B_{12} and other B vitamins. Corn Muffins (page 49) would be a great accompaniment to this savory breakfast dish.

SERVES 3 OR 4

1 tablespoon extra-virgin olive oil

2 cups coarsely chopped collard greens

1 cup cut green beans, in 1-inch pieces

1 cup coarsely chopped scallions (white and green parts) or red onion

⅔ cup steamed corn kernels

1 teaspoon turmeric

14 to 16 ounces soft tofu, cut into ½-inch cubes

½ cup coarsely chopped cilantro

¼ cup nutritional yeast flakes

1 tablespoon tamari

Heat the oil in a medium-size skillet over medium heat. Add the collard greens, green beans, scallions, corn, and turmeric and sauté, stirring occasionally, for 3 to 5 minutes, until the vegetables brighten in color and become fragrant. Gently stir in the tofu and cook for about 3 minutes, until the tofu takes on a yellow hue. Stir in the cilantro and cook for 1 minute. Turn off the heat and stir in the yeast and tamari. Taste and adjust the seasonings if desired. Serve immediately.

Variations

❧ As the seasons change, replace the collard greens with whatever greens are freshest and most vibrant: spinach, tatsoi, chard, or even broccoli.

❧ Substitute mushrooms, summer squash, zucchini, or asparagus for the greens and green beans.

❧ To take the flavor in a different direction, add a few cloves of chopped garlic when you sauté the vegetables, and substitute basil for the cilantro.

Miso Watercress Soup

Miso soup is a nice way to start your day, and is so good for you too. Miso enhances your immune system and has other health benefits. Just be sure not to boil it, or you'll miss out on its digestive enzymes. You can easily build a meal around the soup; serve it alongside cooked brown rice or a combination of millet and amaranth, or enjoy it with boiled eggs, scrambled tofu, or savory muffins, such as Corn Muffins (page 49).

SERVES 3 OR 4

4 cups water

1 (3-inch) piece of dulse

1 bunch of watercress, chopped

14 ounces tofu, cut into bite-size pieces (optional)

1 to 2 tablespoons miso

Sliced scallions (white and green parts), for garnish (optional)

Put the water and dulse in a medium-size saucepan over medium-high heat. Bring to a simmer, then lower the heat and simmer for 5 minutes. Add the watercress and tofu and cook for just a minute or two, until the watercress takes on a brighter green color and the tofu is heated through.

Dissolve the miso in a bit of the hot broth, then stir it into the soup. Add more miso if you prefer a saltier broth. Serve immediately, topped with scallions if you like.

Variations

- Use Bragg Liquid Aminos or tamari instead of the miso. Start with 1 tablespoon and add more to taste.
- Add 1 to 2 tablespoons of grated fresh ginger.
- Substitute kale, collard greens, Chinese cabbage, bok choy, or fresh nettles (see page 96) for the watercress.

CHAPTER 4

main course sensations

The most delicious meals are made with the freshest ingredients (local and organic as much as possible), a joyful mind, an open heart, and a sense of adventure. In this chapter, you'll find a wide variety of colorful and tasty main dishes, from simple to elaborate. Most are easy to make, and all are highly nutritious and completely satisfying.

Beyond using seasonal produce, there are other important ways to cook with the seasons. When it's hot out, you'll probably prefer lighter fare, like Summer Pasta and Bean Salad (page 67), Soba with Tempeh and Broccoli in Coconut Sauce (page 68), or Quick Miso Soup with Nettles and Spicy Thai Noodles (page 96). These quick-cooking meals are an eco-friendly choice too, as they won't heat up your kitchen so much or make your air conditioner work overtime. Another great choice for warm weather is versatile vegetarian nori rolls—the topic of chapter 5.

When winter's chill sets in, it's the perfect time to make long-cooking stews and baked dishes. Not only will they warm you from the inside out, they'll also help heat your home. This is the perfect time of year for dishes like Roasted Vegetable and Quinoa Casserole (page 70), Savory Stuffed Winter Squash (page 72), Shiitake and Kale Lasagna with Marinated Dried Tomatoes and Chèvre (page 74), or a variety of grain-based loaves (pages 76, 77, and 78).

This chapter also includes a bounty of flavorful stews from around the world that are fulfilling any time of year. Look to quicker-cooking stews when the weather is warm, and when it gets chilly, fill your home with the enticing aromas of a long-simmering stew. Either way, you can round out the meal with a green salad and a simple grain dish from chapter 6, either on the side or as a base for the stew. Corn muffins (page 49), Amaranth and Corn Flatbread (page 141), or Corn Fritters (page 140) also make nice accompaniments for most of these dishes.

And remember that you can always put together a great meal by combining several side dishes, or by serving a simple grain dish with sautéed or stir-fried veggies and a sauce. Check out chapters 6 and 7 for recommendations—or go wild in the kitchen and create your own seasonal meals using the recipes in those chapters as your basic building blocks. This is a fun way to cook: going to the market and choosing whatever looks freshest and most appealing, then combining that bounty of fresh produce with staples to create meals that reflect the seasons, your preferences, and your creativity. By playing with all of these variables, you never have to settle for the same meal twice!

Summer Pasta and Bean Salad

This Mediterranean-inspired salad is light and refreshing, yet satisfying enough to serve as the centerpiece of the meal. For a nice summertime lunch or dinner, serve it atop of a bed of garden greens, with Amaranth and Corn Flatbread (page 141) on the side.

SERVES ABOUT 6

12 ounces brown rice spirals or penne

2 cups cooked chickpeas (see page 80)

1 cup sliced carrots

1 cup cut green beans, in 1-inch pieces

1 cup chopped red onion

1 cup minced fresh dill

1 cup freshly squeezed lemon juice

⅓ cup extra-virgin olive oil

¼ cup capers, rinsed

1 teaspoon sea salt

Cook the pasta in a generous amount of boiling water until just tender. Drain and rinse in cold water.

Transfer the pasta to a large bowl. Add the remaining ingredients and gently stir until evenly combined. Taste and adjust the seasonings if desired. Serve at room temperature.

Mediterranean Two-Bean Salad: Substitute other beans, such as navy beans, for the pasta.

Soba with Tempeh and Broccoli in Coconut Sauce

Most varieties of tempeh are gluten-free, but occasionally you'll come across a multigrain version or another type that contains gluten, so check the label to be sure. This is of even greater concern with soba; many varieties use a combination of buckwheat and wheat flour, so read the ingredients to be sure you're getting 100% buckwheat soba.

SERVES ABOUT 4

8 ounces tempeh, cubed

1 (14-ounce) can coconut milk

1 cup coarsely chopped onion

8 ounces 100% soba noodles

2 cups coarsely chopped broccoli

1 tablespoon grated fresh ginger

2 tablespoons chickpea or adzuki bean miso

Put the tempeh, coconut milk, and onion in a large saucepan over medium-high heat. Bring to a boil, then lower the heat, cover, and simmer for about 15 minutes, until the onion is translucent.

Meanwhile, cook the soba noodles in a generous amount of boiling water until just tender. Drain and rinse in cold water.

Add the broccoli and ginger to the tempeh and stir to combine. Simmer for about 5 minutes, until the broccoli is bright green or tender to your liking. Stir the miso into some of the hot broth to form a paste, then stir it back into the tempeh mixture.

Gently stir the soba into the sauce. Serve immediately.

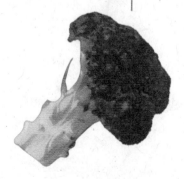

Brown Rice Spirals in Tomato Sauce with Cauliflower, Olives, and Capers

Dulse is an unusual addition to a red sauce, but it's tasty and also helps balance the acidity of the tomatoes. Substitute 1 teaspoon of sea salt for the dulse if you like, or if you don't have any dulse on hand. For a divine meal, top this dish with grated Manchego or your favorite cheese. Of course, you can serve this sauce with any type of pasta you like, but I think it pairs well with spirals—especially the brown rice spirals made by Tinkyada. Or think outside the box and try the sauce over kasha or other cooked grains.

SERVES ABOUT 8

1 tablespoon extra-virgin olive oil

7 cloves garlic, pressed, or more to taste

6 cups sliced plum tomatoes

1 cup chopped onion

⅓ cup dulse

3 cups cauliflower florets

1 cup pitted whole black olives

¼ cup capers, rinsed

1 pound brown rice spirals

Heat the oil in a soup pot over medium heat. Add the garlic and sauté for about 2 minutes. Stir in the tomatoes, onion, and dulse and cook, stirring occasionally, until hot and bubbling. Lower the heat, cover, and simmer for about 10 minutes. Stir in the cauliflower, olives, and capers and simmer for 15 to 20 minutes, until the cauliflower is tender to your liking.

Meanwhile, cook the pasta in a generous amount of boiling water until just tender. Drain and rinse in cold water.

Taste the sauce and adjust the seasonings if you like, then pour it over the pasta and stir gently. Serve immediately.

Roasted Vegetable and Quinoa Casserole

This recipe features a somewhat unusual method of cooking grains. The quinoa is roasted with root vegetables, garlic, and basil, infusing it with their rich flavors. Make this colorful and tasty casserole on a cold day, when the heat of the oven will help warm your house. Red quinoa is particularly attractive in this dish, but if you can't find it, "plain" tan quinoa will do just fine. If you've never tried celeriac, which tastes like celery, this dish is a great way to get acquainted with it. It's a good winter keeper and can be stored for months in the refrigerator or root cellar. To prepare it, simply cut away the tough, knobby skin and then cook it like a potato.

SERVES 4 TO 6

4 cups cubed butternut squash

3 cups cubed beets

2½ cups cubed celeriac

1 cup red quinoa, rinsed

6 cloves garlic, coarsely chopped

3 tablespoons extra-virgin olive oil

2 tablespoons dried basil

1 teaspoon sea salt

1½ cups water

8 ounces crumbled chèvre or feta (optional)

Preheat the oven to 400°F.

Combine the squash, beets, celeriac, quinoa, garlic, oil, basil, and salt in a large casserole dish. Pour in the water, cover, and bake for 45 to 50 minutes, until the vegetables are tender to your liking. Serve immediately, topped with the chèvre if you like.

Savory Stuffed Winter Squash

A perfect offering on any cool autumn evening, this flavorful dish is so satisfying and festive that it can serve as the centerpiece for Thanksgiving or any holiday meal. Delicata, sweet dumpling, acorn, and butternut squash all work equally well with the delicious stuffing which also makes a side dish, with or without the cheese. As always, I recommend a local, artisanal cheese, preferably made with goat's or sheep's milk or milk from grass-fed cows. The Jade Pearl rice stuffing is so delicious and attractive that you could forgo the squash and serve it on its own—or beef it up by adding French green lentils, as in the variation below.

Jade Rice Pilaf with French Lentils and Toasted Walnuts: Forgo the squash. While the rice is simmering, cook ½ cup of French green lentils in a generous amount of boiling water, along with 2 bay leaves. When the lentils are tender (about 20 minutes), drain them and discard the bay leaves. Stir the lentils into the rice when you add the thyme and sage. Serve as is, or topped with the cheese if you like.

SERVES ABOUT 6

3 medium winter squash

⅓ cup chopped walnuts

1 tablespoon extra-virgin olive oil

½ cup diced red onion

¼ cup diced celery

1 clove garlic, minced

1¼ cups Jade Pearl rice

¾ cup diced red bell pepper

¼ teaspoon sea salt

2½ cups boiling water

1 tablespoon fresh thyme leaves

½ teaspoon chopped fresh sage

2 cups grated Gouda or Cheddar cheese (about 8 ounces)

Preheat the oven to 400°F.

Leave the squash whole. Place them in a baking pan and bake for about 1 hour, until tender; an inserted fork should go into the center of the squash easily.

Meanwhile, toast the walnuts in a large dry saucepan over medium heat, stirring often, for about 5 minutes, until they begin to smell fragrant. Add the oil, onion, celery, and garlic. Sauté, stirring occasionally, for about 5 minutes, until the onion begins to soften. Add the rice, bell pepper, and salt and cook, stirring occasionally, for 2 to 3 minutes. Lower the heat, then slowly pour in the water. Cover and simmer for about 20 minutes, until all of the water is absorbed.

Stir in the thyme and sage. Taste and adjust the seasonings if desired.

Cut the squash in half lengthwise, and scoop out the seeds. Fill the squash halves with the rice mixture. Top with the cheese and serve immediately.

Variations

❧ Jade Pearl rice is both delicious and attractive in this pilaf, but you can certainly substitute other varieties of rice, such as long-grain brown rice or basmati; or, for more color and flair, try Bhutanese red rice or black forbidden rice. Just remember that when substituting other varieties of rice, you may need to adjust the cooking time (see page 27).

Shiitake and Kale Lasagna with Marinated Dried Tomatoes and Chèvre

A feast! You can use rice lasagna noodles in any lasagna recipe (those made by Pastariso are especially good). In fact, even though I don't follow a gluten-free diet, I prefer rice pasta to whole wheat. Here, I've used chèvre instead of ricotta, and replaced the mozzarella with Cheddar (hopefully a local artisanal variety made with goat's milk or milk from grass-fed cows) for a delicious and unusual variation. For more flavor, use chèvre with basil or other Italian herbs.

SERVES 4 TO 6

½ cup water

2 cups Tomato Sauce with Fennel and Marinated Dried Tomatoes (page 152) or other prepared pasta sauce

8 ounces uncooked rice lasagna noodles

6 ounces chèvre

1½ cups coarsely chopped kale

1 cup stemmed and coarsely chopped shiitake mushrooms

½ cup Marinated Dried Tomatoes (page 171)

2 cups grated Cheddar cheese (about 8 ounces)

Preheat the oven to 400°F.

Put the water and ½ cup of the tomato sauce in an 8-inch square baking dish and spread it over the bottom of the dish. Arrange a single layer of noodles over the sauce. Spread or crumble the chèvre on top of the noodles. Top with another layer of noodles and then all of the kale. Scatter the mushrooms and dried tomatoes over the kale. Place a final layer of noodles over the vegetables and press down gently. Pour the remaining 1½ cups sauce over the noodles and spread it evenly, then top with the grated cheese.

Cover with foil (shiny side down) or a baking sheet and bake for about 45 minutes, until the noodles are soft and the lasagna is bubbling hot. Let it stand for about 10 minutes to set up. Cut into squares and serve immediately.

Variations

❧ Swap other kinds of fresh mushrooms for the shiitakes: white button mushrooms, criminis, portobellos, or wild mushrooms, such as chanterelles.

❧ Use other shapes of pasta, like penne or spirals. If you do this, you can select from a wider range of gluten-free pastas, such as quinoa-corn pasta or multigrain varieties.

❧ Replace the sauce in this recipe with 2 cups of the sauce in Brown Rice Spirals in Tomato Sauce with Cauliflower, Olives, and Capers (page 69).

Teff Loaf with Red Bell Peppers and African Spices

Teff revisits its Ethiopian roots in this recipe, where it's cooked with traditional vegetables and spices. Beyond being delicious, slices of this loaf are beautiful, with a colorful mosaic pattern. Ethiopian Sunshine Stew (page 84) is the perfect partner for this dish.

SERVES 6 TO 8

2 teaspoons fenugreek seeds

1 teaspoon cumin seeds

1 teaspoon coriander seeds

5 whole cloves

3 tablespoons extra-virgin olive oil

1 cup chopped onion

4 cloves garlic, pressed

1½ cups teff

1 teaspoon dried chile flakes

4½ cups boiling water

1½ cups diced red bell pepper

1 teaspoon sea salt

Toast the fenugreek seeds, cumin seeds, coriander seeds, and cloves in a small dry skillet over medium heat, stirring often, for about 1 minute, until fragrant. Transfer to a spice grinder or seed mill and grind until powdery.

Heat the oil in a large soup pot over medium heat. Add the onion, garlic, teff, and chile flakes and sauté for 3 to 5 minutes, until the teff is coated with the oil and the aroma of garlic and chiles fills the air. Lower the heat, then slowly pour in the water. Stir in the ground spices, bell pepper, and salt. Cover and simmer for about 20 minutes, until the teff is tender and all of the water is absorbed. Taste and adjust the seasonings if desired.

Pour the mixture into a standard loaf pan and let stand for about 30 minutes, until set up. Slice into pieces about 1 inch thick and serve immediately. If you don't want to wait, you can serve scoops of the mixture piping hot. It will have a texture like mashed potatoes, as it only sets up after cooling a bit.

Red Lentil and Teff Loaf with Red Wine and Porcini Sauce

I made this fantastic egg- and dairy-free loaf for a summer wedding that I catered and everyone loved it, even though most of the guests weren't vegan. And while the final product is impressive, it's quite easy to put together. Yellow-skinned summer squash adds eye appeal to the loaf, but zucchini would also work just fine.

SERVES 6 TO 8

⅔ cup red lentils, rinsed

½ cup teff

2½ cups water

2 tablespoons extra-virgin olive oil

5 garlic scapes, chopped, or 5 cloves garlic, chopped

2 cups yellow summer squash, halved lengthwise and sliced into half-moons

1 teaspoon sea salt

2 cups chopped scallions (white and green parts)

1 cup coarsely chopped fresh basil leaves

1¼ cups Red Wine and Porcini Sauce (page 150)

Put the lentils, teff, and water in a large saucepan over high heat. Bring to a boil, then lower the heat, cover, and simmer for 15 to 20 minutes, until the teff is tender and the lentils have practically dissolved.

Meanwhile, heat the oil in a large skillet over medium heat. Add the garlic scapes, squash, and salt and sauté for about 3 minutes, until the color of the squash brightens.

Add the sauté to the cooked lentils, along with the scallions and basil, and stir well, and continue cooking until all of the water is absorbed. Taste and adjust the seasonings if desired.

Pour the mixture into a standard loaf pan and let it cool for about 30 minutes, until it sets up. Slice into pieces about 1 inch thick and serve immediately, topping each slice with a few tablespoons of the sauce.

Kasha Loaf with Walnuts and Sunflower Seeds

Kasha is simply toasted buckwheat groats, and if you like, you can make your own at home. Just toast the buckwheat groats in a dry pan in a 375°F oven for about 20 minutes, and you're good to go. For a special touch, serve this loaf topped with Red Wine and Porcini Sauce (page 150) or Mushroom-Leek Sauce (page 151). It would make an especially lovely meal if you start with Shiitake Soup with Cashew Cream (page 144) or Tomato-Lentil Stew with Kale (page 146) as a first course.

Soaking Nuts and Seeds

There's debate about the merits of soaking nuts and seeds before eating them or using them in cooking. Many avid raw food enthusiast maintain that nuts and seeds (except hazelnuts, Brazil nuts, and hempseeds), are difficult to digest, and that soaking helps with this. You might experiment with presoaking and see whether you notice any difference.

To presoak nuts or seeds, just put them in a bowl or jar and pour in three parts water per part of nuts or seeds. Let them soak overnight or for at least 12 hours. Then drain them and rinse them well.

If you'll be using the nuts or seeds right away, you're good to go. If you've soaked a lot and want to save them for later, you have two options: You can toast them in a low oven or food dehydrator until they're dry and crunchy. Alternatively, you can store them in the refrigerator; if you go this route, it's a good idea to rinse them once a day.

SERVES 6 TO 8

1⅓ cups kasha

¼ teaspoon sea salt

2⅔ cups boiling water

1 tablespoon extra-virgin olive oil

1 cup diced onion

4 cloves garlic, sliced

1 cup diced celery

1 cup diced red bell pepper

¾ cup walnuts

½ cup raw sunflower seeds

½ cup quinoa flour

1 teaspoon dried sage, or 1 tablespoon minced fresh sage

1½ teaspoons dried thyme, or 1½ tablespoons fresh thyme leaves

1 tablespoon umeboshi paste or miso

Preheat the oven to 375°F. Lightly oil a standard loaf pan or a medium-size casserole dish.

Toast the kasha and salt in a medium-size dry saucepan or skillet (one with a tight-fitting lid) over medium heat, stirring often, for about 2 minutes, until the kasha is heated through and aromatic. Lower the heat, then slowly pour in the boiling water. Cover and simmer for about 10 minutes, until all of the water is absorbed.

Meanwhile, heat the oil in a large skillet over medium-high heat. Add the onion and garlic and sauté for about 5 minutes, until the onion begins to soften. Add the celery and sauté for about 3 minutes, until the celery becomes bright green. Add the bell pepper and sauté for 3 to 5 minutes, until its color brightens. Transfer the sautéed veggies to a large mixing bowl.

Grind the walnuts into a flour in a food processor (see page 24), then add them to the veggie mixture. Grind the sunflower seeds into a flour in the food processor and transfer them to the bowl as well. Add the cooked kasha, along with the quinoa flour, sage, thyme, and umeboshi paste and stir until thoroughly combined. You may want to start with a spoon, but at some point, it will be easier and more fun to use your hands. Taste and adjust the seasonings if desired.

Transfer the mixture to the prepared pan, cover, and bake for 30 minutes. Turn off the oven, uncover the pan, and let the loaf sit in the warm oven for 20 to 30 minutes. Slice into pieces about 1 inch thick and serve immediately.

Cooking Beans from Scratch

Some beans cook faster if presoaked; others can be cooked on a whim. Most small beans, such as mung beans and lentils cook relatively quickly without any presoaking. Soak medium-size beans, such as black, pinto, kidney, lima, and navy, for at least 4 hours before cooking. Chickpeas and soybeans need at least 6 hours. For a quick soak method, cover beans with boiling water (triple the amount of beans) and soak for 1 hour, then drain and rinse.

Before soaking, pick through a measured amount of beans and discard any defective beans, stones, or other debris. Then rinse the beans at least three times. If they need presoaking, put them in a pot or large bowl with triple the volume of water.

Always discard the soaking water; this will get rid of some of the gas-producing compounds. Then rinse the beans until the water runs clear. To further help with digestion and gas, cook beans with a sea vegetable. Dulse and kelp are good choices. They'll also enhance the flavor of the beans and add nutrients.

The proportion of beans to cooking liquid depends on whether you want the beans to be whole, soft, or creamy. Three parts liquid to one part beans is usually a good starting point. For whole beans suitable for a salad or side dish, use a bit less, for a creamier final result, you might use more.

The actual cooking couldn't be simpler: Just put the beans, sea vegetable, and cooking liquid in a pot and put the pot over high heat. When it comes to a boil, give it a quick stir, then lower the heat, cover, and simmer until the beans are tender. Cooking time varies from just 15 minutes for red lentils to 3 hours for soybeans. Even for a particular type of bean, cooking time can vary depending on how old and dried-out the beans are. Here's a quick rundown of cooking time for beans used in this book: Black beans, navy beans, and pintos all take about 1½ hours, and chickpeas usually take about 3 hours. You can shorten the cooking time if you use a pressure cooker.

Corn Grits with Sautéed Onion, Kale, and Cheddar

I used to make this quick and easy dish for my daughter after her Ultimate Frisbee practice. I'd start it when she walked in the door, and it was ready by the time she was out of her shower. I recommend using a raw milk Cheddar here; if you can find a local variety made with goat's milk or milk from grass-fed cows, so much the better. I highly recommend seeking out a high-quality sea salt, such as Hawaiian Deep Sea Salt or Celtic Sea Salt for this dish.

SERVES 3 TO 4

2 tablespoons extra-virgin olive oil

1 cup sliced red onion

1 cup stemmed and sliced shiitake mushrooms

½ teaspoon sea salt

3 cups chopped kale

⅔ cup corn grits

1 teaspoon dried thyme

2 cups boiling water

1¼ cups grated Cheddar cheese (about 5 ounces)

Heat the oil in a large saucepan or skillet (one with a tight-fitting lid) over medium-high heat. Add the onion and sauté for about 5 minutes, until it begins to soften. Add the mushrooms and salt and sauté for about 5 minutes, until the mushrooms soften. Stir in the kale, grits, and thyme. Lower the heat, then slowly pour in the water. Cover and simmer for 5 to 10 minutes, until all of the water is absorbed.

Add the cheese, cover, and let sit for about 3 minutes, until the cheese melts. Use the edge of a spatula to cut the dish into wedges. Serve immediately.

African-Spiced Teff and Lentil Stew with Collard Greens and Yams

When I teach my Vegetarian Express cooking class, I include this recipe, which is often the first taste of teff for many of my students. Since teff is native to Ethiopia, cooking it with African spices gives it an authentic and robust flavor. Here, the combination with quick-cooking red lentils and coconut milk makes for a fabulous, rich-tasting stew with a great nutritional profile.

SERVES 4 TO 6

⅔ cup red lentils, rinsed

⅔ cup teff

2 cups peeled, grated yams

¼ cup seeded, chopped poblano pepper

1 teaspoon cumin seeds

1 teaspoon ground fenugreek

1 (14-ounce) can coconut milk

2¼ cups water

7 cups sliced collard greens

1¾ cups diced tomatoes

3 tablespoons grated fresh ginger

1 teaspoon sea salt

Combine the lentils, teff, yams, poblano, cumin seeds, and fenugreek in a soup pot. Add the coconut milk. Pour some of the water into the coconut milk can and swish it around, then pour it into the pan; if needed, repeat with more of the water so you get every last drop of the coconut milk's goodness into the pan. Stir everything together, then bring to a boil over medium-high heat. Lower the heat, cover, and simmer for 15 to 20 minutes, until the lentils practically dissolve and the teff is tender.

Add the collard greens, tomatoes, ginger, and salt and simmer for about 5 minutes, until the collards are bright green. Taste and adjust the seasonings if desired.

Butternut Squash and Tempeh Stew with Shiitake Mushrooms

The cooked butternut squash practically melts to form a sweet sauce in this warming stew. Chickpea miso is especially complementary to the flavors of this stew, but you can substitute other gluten-free varieties if you like; hearty brown rice, adzuki bean, or millet miso would all be good choices. You can use either red or white wine in this dish—or any other wine for that matter. I recommend using whatever wine you'd like to drink with the stew. For a special treat, try pear or peach wine.

SERVES 4 TO 6

½ cup dried shiitake mushrooms, stemmed

⅔ cup wine

2 tablespoons extra-virgin olive oil

1 pound tempeh, cubed

4 cups cubed butternut squash

4 cups cubed potatoes

1½ cups water

2 tablespoons chickpea miso

2 tablespoons prepared mustard

1 teaspoon dried rosemary

1½ teaspoons dried thyme

1 teaspoon dried sage

Soak the shiitake mushrooms in the wine for about 15 minutes, until they soften.

Heat the oil in a soup pot over medium heat. Add the tempeh and cook, stirring occasionally, for 5 to 10 minutes, until golden brown. Add the squash, potatoes, water, wine, and mushrooms. (You may want cut the mushrooms into bite-size pieces or at least halve larger mushrooms.) Bring to a boil, then lower the heat, cover, and simmer for about 20 minutes, until the potatoes are tender and the butternut squash is melting into the pot.

Stir the miso and mustard into some of the hot broth, then stir the mixture back into the stew, along with the rosemary, thyme, and sage.

Ethiopian Sunshine Stew

This warming and stimulating stew is one of my favorite winter meals because it tastes like a trip to a sunny climate and keeps the cold at bay. In this recipe the spices are first sautéed in ghee to trap their volatile oils, then the chickpeas are cooked from scratch together with these spices to infuse them with rich, complex flavors. Long, slow cooking sweetens the cabbage and carrots and makes them practically melt in your mouth. For a hearty main dish, serve the stew over millet or Bhutanese red rice. You need to soak the chickpeas for at least six hours, and then the stew cooks for over an hour, so plan ahead.

Variations

- For a vegan version, substitute ¼ cup extra-virgin olive or sunflower oil for the ghee.

- Onions and garlic make a lovely addition; simply add chopped onions and garlic when you add the carrots and cabbage.

- For a greener stew with a higher iron content, substitute collard greens or kale for half of the cabbage, adding either one about 15 minutes after you add the cabbage and carrots.

SERVES ABOUT 8

2 teaspoons cumin seeds

1 teaspoon fenugreek seeds

½ teaspoon coriander seeds

¼ teaspoon whole allspice

½ teaspoon ground ginger

½ teaspoon ground cardamom

¼ teaspoon ground turmeric

¼ teaspoon ground cloves

¼ cup ghee (see page 86), or ½ cup butter

1 teaspoon dried chile flakes

10 cups water

1½ cups dried chickpeas, sorted and soaked for 6 to 8 hours

7 cups coarsely chopped cabbage

2½ cups coarsely chopped carrots

1 tablespoon sea salt

Toast the cumin seeds, fenugreek seeds, coriander seeds, and allspice in a small dry skillet for about 1 minute, stirring frequently, until fragrant. Transfer to a spice grinder or seed mill, add the ginger, cardamom, turmeric, and cloves, and grind until powdery.

Drain and rinse the chickpeas.

Put the ghee in a large soup pot over medium heat. Once it melts, add the chile flakes and ground spices and sauté for about 1 minute, until the chile flakes take on a brighter hue. Stir in the water and chickpeas. Turn up the heat to high and bring to a boil, then lower the heat, cover, and simmer for about 30 minutes, until the chickpeas begin to soften.

Add the cabbage and carrots and simmer for about 30 more minutes, until the cabbage is transparent and practically melts into the broth.

Stir in the salt. Taste and adjust the seasonings if desired.

85

Making Ghee

Even if you aren't familiar with ghee, an ingredient commonly used in Indian cooking, you may be familiar with clarified butter. In fact, the two are one and the same. No matter what name it goes by, it couldn't be simpler to make; the method basically boils down to heating butter until the solids separate out, so that you can pour off the clear butterfat; this is the ghee or clarified butter. It's a useful ingredient to keep around for several reasons. It has a higher smoke point than butter, so it can be used for sautéing and other higher heat applications without burning. It also keeps better than regular butter.

Here's how you make it: Place 1 pound of unsalted butter in a small saucepan and heat it gently over low heat until it melts. Allow it to simmer for about 10 minutes, scooping off the foam from time to time. Remove the saucepan from the heat and let it stand for a few minutes so all of the solids can settle to the bottom. Then carefully pour off the clear liquid, leaving the solids in the pot. It's a good idea to pour the ghee through a fine-mesh sieve to ensure all of the solids are filtered out. You may even want to line the sieve with cheesecloth. Store the ghee in an airtight container. Because it keeps so well, you need not store it in the refrigerator. If you keep it in your kitchen cabinet, away from light and tightly sealed, it will last for months.

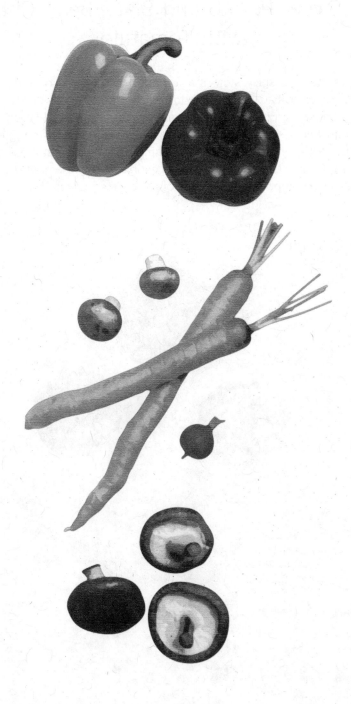

Sweet Potato and Black Bean Chili with Tomatillos

This sweet and spicy stew is a fun and unusual take on chili. And if you happen to have leftovers, it tastes even better a day or two later. If you choose to top the stew with grated cheese, as usual I recommend a local variety—hopefully made with goat's milk or milk from grass-fed cows. Kelp may seem like an unusual ingredient here, but it has several benefits: it makes the beans more digestible, and it also contains flavor-enhancing compounds and loads of minerals and vitamins.

SERVES 6 TO 8

1 cup dried black beans, soaked overnight

1 tablespoon kelp flakes, or 1 (3-inch) piece of kelp

4 cups water

1 teaspoon ground cinnamon, or 1 cinnamon stick

1 cayenne pepper, seeded and minced, or 1 teaspoon dried chile flakes

2 tablespoons extra-virgin coconut oil

1½ cups chopped red onions

3 cups peeled, grated sweet potatoes

4 cups quartered tomatillos

3½ cups diced tomatoes

4 cups fresh or frozen corn kernels

1½ cups tightly packed chopped cilantro

2 cloves garlic, pressed

1½ teaspoons ground cumin

1½ teaspoons sea salt

Grated Cheddar cheese (optional), for garnish

Drain and rinse the beans, then put them in a large soup pot with the kelp, water, cinnamon, and cayenne. Bring to a boil over high heat, then lower the heat, cover, and simmer.

Heat the oil in a medium-size skillet over medium heat. Add the onions and sweet potatoes and sauté over medium heat for about 10 minutes, until the sweet potatoes soften and take on a brighter orange color. Add the sauté to the soup pot and continue to simmer for about 45 minutes, until the beans are soft.

Stir in the tomatillos and tomatoes. Simmer for about 10 minutes, until the tomatillos almost melt into the stew. Stir in the corn, cilantro, garlic, cumin, and salt. Taste and adjust the seasonings if desired. Serve topped with the cheese if you like.

Coconut Curry Lentil and Millet Stew

This sweet golden stew is very satisfying and warming, making it the perfect choice for a chilly night. Ginger and cilantro enhance the Indian accent and also boost the immune system and energize digestion. Mineral-rich dulse provides similar benefits, and if you're leery of sea vegetables, no worries; it dissolves into the soup so you won't even notice it in every loving spoonful. For an amazing winter meal, serve the stew with Spiced Yams with Pecans (page 139) and end the meal with Honey Hazelnut Treats (page 181) or Maple Sugar Cookies (page 179) .

SERVES ABOUT 6

1 cup red lentils, rinsed

1 cup millet, rinsed

4 cups cubed delicata squash

2 tablespoons curry powder

2 tablespoons dulse

2 (14-ounce) cans coconut milk

3½ cups water

1 cup chopped cilantro

1½ teaspoons grated fresh ginger

1 teaspoon sea salt

Combine the lentils, millet, squash, curry powder, and dulse in a soup pot. Add the coconut milk. Pour some of the water into the coconut milk cans and swish them around, then pour into the pot; if needed, repeat with more of the water so you get every last drop of the coconut milk's goodness into the pan. Stir everything together, then bring to a boil over medium-high heat. Lower the heat, cover, and simmer for about 20 minutes, until the lentils practically dissolve and the millet is tender.

Stir in the cilantro, ginger, and salt. Taste and adjust the seasonings if desired.

Coconut Curry Lentil Teff Loaf: Pour the cooked stew into a 9 by 13-inch baking pan or 2 standard loaf pans and let it set for about 30 minutes for it to set up, then slice and serve.

Variations

❧ Use an assortment of vegetables for a total of 4 cups, such as onions, carrots, potatoes, sweet potatoes, and bell peppers.

❧ You can make this stew in a pressure cooker. Combine the lentils, millet, squash, coconut milk, curry powder, dulse, coconut milk, and water in a 6-quart pressure cooker and stir them together. Lock the lid and bring the cooker up to pressure over high heat. Adjust the heat to maintain high pressure and cook for 10 minutes. Allow the pressure to come down naturally, which will take about 10 minutes; if you're in a hurry, put the pressure cooker in the sink and run cold water over it. Stir in the cilantro, ginger, and salt.

South American Quinoa Stew

This dish boasts sharp and sweet tomatillos, pungent garlic, and spicy chiles, making it comforting and stimulating in every bite. Served with Amaranth and Corn Flatbread (page 141), it makes a perfect meal for a cold winter's night. Chiles can vary tremendously in heat and flavor qualities, and dried chiles extend the range of flavor and textural qualities. For an extremely spicy soup, use a Scotch bonnet, Thai, habanero, or cayenne pepper; for moderately hot, use a serrano; and for mildly hot, use an anaheim, ancho, jalapeño, or poblano and remove the seeds from the chiles.

SERVES 6 TO 8

1 tablespoon cumin seeds

2 tablespoons extra-virgin olive oil

1 cup coarsely chopped onion

1 cup quinoa, rinsed

8 cups water

4 cups diced potatoes, in ½-inch cubes

3 cups diced yams, in ½-inch cubes

1 chile pepper, dried or fresh, seeded and chopped

2 teaspoons sea salt

2 teaspoons ground cumin

2 cups diced tomatillos

½ cup coarsely chopped cilantro

8 small cloves garlic, pressed

Toast the cumin seeds in a large soup pot over medium heat, stirring often, for about 1 minute, until fragrant. Add the oil, onion, and quinoa and sauté for about 5 minutes, until the onion begins to soften. Add the water, potatoes, and yams, then stir in the chile pepper, salt, and ground cumin. Bring to a boil over high heat, then lower the heat, cover, and simmer for 15 to 20 minutes, until the potatoes are soft.

Stir in the tomatillos, cilantro, and garlic. Taste and adjust the seasonings if desired.

Variation

*§ For a soup that will deliver more long-lasting energy, omit the potatoes and increase the amount of yams to 7 cups.

Garlicky Peanut Soup

In this creamy and spicy main course soup, onions, carrots, parsnips, and cabbage combine with warming spices to create a fusion of heat and sweet that will sustain you through the coldest night of the year. For a delicious and filling meal, ladle the hot soup over cooked brown rice, millet, or teff.

SERVES 6 TO 8

1 teaspoon fenugreek seeds

1 teaspoon coriander seeds

2 tablespoons extra-virgin olive oil, extra-virgin coconut oil, or ghee (see page 86)

1 cup coarsely chopped onion

8 cups coarsely chopped cabbage

4 cups coarsely chopped parsnips

3½ cups diced tomatoes

1 cup coarsely chopped carrots

2 cups cooked chickpeas (see page 80)

1 teaspoon dried chile flakes

½ teaspoon ground nutmeg, preferably freshly grated

¼ teaspoon ground cloves

4½ cups hot water

1 cup peanut butter (see page 24)

1½ tablespoons sea salt

1 head of garlic, pressed

Toast the fenugreek and coriander seeds in a large soup pot over medium heat, stirring often, for about 2 minutes, until fragrant. Transfer to a spice grinder or seed mill and grind until powdery.

Heat the oil in the same pot over medium heat. Add the onion and sauté for about 5 minutes, until the onion begins to soften. Add the cabbage, parsnips, tomatoes, and carrots and sauté a moment longer, then stir in the chickpeas, chile flakes, nutmeg, and cloves, 2½ cups of the hot water, and the ground fenugreek and coriander. Bring to a boil, then lower the heat to maintain a simmer.

Put the peanut butter and the remaining 2 cups hot water in a blender and puree until creamy. Pour the mixture into the soup, then stir in the salt. Cover and simmer for about 1 hour, until the cabbage is tender to your liking.

Stir in the garlic and simmer for 5 minutes to blend the flavors. Taste and adjust the seasonings if desired.

Variation

- Substitute cooked lentils for the chickpeas.
- Substitute sweet potatoes, yams, or butternut squash for the parsnips.

Quick Miso Soup with Nettles and Spicy Thai Noodles

If you have nettles growing in your area and feel confident that you can identify them, you're in for a treat. They will awaken your palate and energize your spirit. Harvest them in spring or early summer, before they flower, removing just the top few inches so the nettles can regenerate. Be sure to wear gloves when harvesting and working with them so they don't sting you. (Don't worry; they lose this power when cooked.) The spicy noodles add a spark that complements the bright green flavor of the nettles, which is somewhat similar to fresh peas. If you don't have nettles, see the variations below for substitutions.

Variations

- No nettles? No problem! Just substitute 1 to 2 cups of peas, spinach, mizuna, tatsoi, bok choy, watercress, or mustard greens.

- To boost this healthful soup's immune-enhancing effects, add about 1 cup of stemmed and sliced fresh shiitakes; they'll also lend a buttery flavor to the soup.

- Use other noodles, such as bean thread or 100% buckwheat soba, in place of the rice vermicelli. Or substitute 2 cups of cooked rice.

- Substitute basil oil or garlic oil for the chili oil.

- Garnish with strips of toasted nori.

SERVES ABOUT 4

5 to 8 ounces of rice vermicelli

6 cups water

4 cups fresh nettle tops

2 cups finely chopped broccoli

2 cups diced tofu

½ cup coarsely chopped chives or scallions (white and green parts)

2 cloves pressed garlic

¼ cup miso, or more to taste

1 to 2 tablespoons hot chili oil

1 to 2 tablespoons tamari

Put the rice vermicelli in a medium-size bowl and pour in boiling water to cover. Test occasionally and drain the noodles once they're soft, usually about 10 minutes. Rinse with cold water, and set aside to drain completely.

Meanwhile, put the water and nettles in a soup pot over high heat. Bring to a boil, then turn down the heat to medium-low. Stir in the broccoli, tofu, and chives and simmer for 5 to 10 minutes, until the broccoli is tender to your liking and the nettles are bright green. Stir in the garlic.

Dissolve the miso in a small amount of the hot broth, then stir it into the soup. Taste and add more miso or garlic if desired.

Heat the chili oil and tamari in a large skillet over medium-high heat. Add the noodles and sauté for 1 to 3 minutes, until the noodles are evenly coated and well seasoned.

Ladle the hot soup into bowls, mound the noodles on top, and serve immediately.

CHAPTER 5

sushi party

If you think sushi is all about raw fish, think again. The word "sushi" is actually an umbrella term that refers to a variety of foods based on cold cooked rice pressed into different shapes. The type of sushi made in this chapter might more properly be called nori rolls, but why quibble? I just call it delectable. The first time I had it was back in the late 1970s, when I was studying creative arts in education in Boulder, Colorado, and some new friends invited me to join them for lunch. They served brown rice and vegetables wrapped in toasted nori with a spicy wasabi dip (aka maki sushi), and I fell in love at first bite.

Maki sushi is nutritious and delicious, and once you've practiced a bit, it's easy to make. It's also beautiful and lends itself to culinary artistry. You can create an endless variety of colorful mosaic patterns by using different varieties of rice—or even a rice medley—and different combinations of filling ingredients. For color and flavor, seasonal vegetables are a must, whether raw, steamed, stir-fried, marinated, or pickled. Including strips of pan-fried tofu, gingered tempeh, or plain omelet completes the protein, while raw and toasted seeds, such as sunflower, pumpkin, sesame, chia, and hemp, will add texture, minerals, and a little more protein.

You may notice that I don't add vinegar and sugar to the rice, as is traditional. I prefer to keep the rice simple, so the flavors of the filling ingredients really shine. This also allows you to enjoy the subtle and unique flavors of the many tasty, exotic varieties of rice we're lucky to have access to these days. Beyond that old standby, short-grain brown rice, you can also use sweet brown rice, Jade Pearl rice, black forbidden rice, Bhutanese red rice, or a combination. This chapter starts with recipes for four different rice fillings, but feel free to experiment with any type of rice you like. Short-grain varieties usually yield the best results, since they tend to cook up sticky, but if you want to try something different, I say go for it! If you want to use a combination other than those in this chapter and need some guidance on cooking them together, see page 27.

However you make them, you'll find that nori rolls are also very versatile fare. They're great for lunch, dinner, or appetizers. Served with a bowl of Miso Watercress Soup (page 64) and Lemony Carrot and Beet Salad (page 111), nori rolls can be the centerpiece of a special dinner party. And because they travel well, they also make great picnic or potluck fare.

When you first start making nori rolls, or if you experiment with long-grain rice, be sure to cook it with about one-third sweet brown rice to help the rice stick together. Otherwise you might end up with a roll that doesn't stick together well or that just doesn't turn out right. Don't despair! Just serve the ingredients artfully arranged in a bowl and call it chirashi sushi (which means "scattered sushi"). No one will be the wiser. In fact, they'll think you're ahead of the curve and onto the next big thing in sushi. Either way, it will still taste delicious.

Short-Grain Brown Rice

Although white sushi rice is traditionally used for making nori rolls, brown rice is nutritionally superior, having more B vitamins and fiber. And unlike long-grain brown rice, which cooks up fluffy, short-grain brown rice has a slight sticky quality that's perfect for nori rolls, especially if you cook it in a pressure cooker as in the variations below.

MAKES ENOUGH
RICE FOR AT LEAST
8 NORI ROLLS

---

2 cups short-grain brown rice, rinsed

4 cups cold water

Pinch of sea salt

Combine the rice, water, and salt in a large saucepan. Bring to a boil over medium-high heat, then lower the heat, cover, and simmer for about 40 minutes, until all of the water is absorbed. Uncover the rice and let it stand for about 1 hour, until cool enough to handle, before making nori rolls. If the rice is too hot, it will steam holes in the nori.

Variations

⚜ Cook the rice with 3 slices of fresh ginger.

⚜ Use 1 cup each of short-grain brown rice and sweet brown rice.

⚜ Swap Jade Pearl rice for the brown rice and decrease the simmering time to 20 minutes.

⚜ To use a pressure cooker with a rice crock instead of a saucepan, decrease the amount of water to 3 cups and cook for about 40 minutes, following the method on page 36.

Exotic Rice Blend

Cooking with black forbidden rice or Bhutanese red rice adds more color to nori rolls, making them a feast for the eyes, as well as the palate.

MAKES ENOUGH
RICE FOR AT LEAST
8 NORI ROLLS

1½ cups black
forbidden rice or
Bhutanese red rice

½ cup sweet brown
rice, rinsed

4 cups cold water

Pinch of sea saltt

Combine the rice, water, and salt in a large saucepan over medium-high heat. Bring to a boil, then lower the heat, cover, and simmer for 30 to 40 minutes, until all of the water is absorbed. Uncover the rice and let it stand for about 1 hour, until cool enough to handle, before making nori rolls.

Variations

⚜ To use a pressure cooker with a rice crock instead of a saucepan, decrease the amount of water to 3 cups and cook for about 30 minutes, following the method on page 36.

Trio of Rice

Enhanced nutrition along with fantastic flavor makes black forbidden rice, Bhutanese red rice, and sweet brown rice a great rice combination. This trio also makes for an attractive mosaic of colors. Nori rolls that pair this rice blend with steamed beets, carrots, and kale are especially delicious.

MAKES ENOUGH
RICE FOR AT LEAST
8 NORI ROLLS

¾ cup black
forbidden rice

¾ cup Bhutanese
red rice

½ cup sweet brown
rice, rinsed

4 cups cold water

Pinch of sea salt

Combine the rice, water, and salt in a large saucepan over medium-high heat. Bring to a boil, then lower the heat, cover, and simmer for 30 to 40 minutes, until all of the water is absorbed. Uncover the rice and let it stand for about 1 hour, until cool enough to handle, before making nori rolls.

Variations

To use a pressure cooker with a rice crock instead of a saucepan, decrease the amount of water to 3 cups and cook for about 30 minutes, following the method on page 36.

Jade Pearl Rice Eco-Cook Method

I came up with this quick cooking method quite by accident and have since used it time and time again. A neighbor called me just as the rice had come to a boil and I needed to go over to her house. I turned off the rice, and when I got back about 30 minutes later, it was cooked to perfection. You could try this method with other quick-cooking grains if you like. Jade Pearl rice is an especially delicious choice for nori rolls filled with Gingered Tempeh and Shiitakes (page 110) and mesclun.

MAKES ENOUGH
RICE FOR AT LEAST
8 NORI ROLLS

---

2 cups Jade Pearl
rice

4 cups water

Pinch of sea salt

Combine the rice, water, and salt in a large saucepan. Cover and bring to a boil over medium-high heat. Boil for about 3 minutes, then turn off the heat and let the residual heat cook the rice. The rice will be ready in 20 to 30 minutes, when all of the water is absorbed. Uncover the rice and let it stand for about 1 hour, until cool enough to handle, before making nori rolls.

Sushi Extravaganza!

The sky's the limit when it comes to fillings for nori rolls. Below you'll find a wide variety of suggestions. Mix and match to your heart's content—and your palate's delight. Rotate the vegetables with the seasons: asparagus in spring, zucchini in summer, cucumber in late summer, daikon radish in the fall, beets in winter... Look for pickled ginger and naturally fermented pickled vegetables such as pickled ginger carrots, red sauerkraut, or cucumber pickles in natural food stores, or make your own using the recipe on page 112. Avoid brightly colored pickled ginger and wasabi; these generally contain food dye.

Protein

- Strips of a plain omelet
- Sunflower, pumpkin, sesame, hemp, or chia seeds, raw or toasted
- Gingered Tempeh and Shiitakes (page 110)

Vegetables

- Asparagus spears, steamed, sautéed, or raw
- Shredded red cabbage
- Shredded daikon radish
- Raw or grilled bell pepper strips
- Chopped raw kale or mustard greens
- Whole leaves of raw mizuna, watercress, or tatsoi
- Avocado slices
- Cucumber, cut into thin spears
- Snow peas, cut into strips
- Scallions or chives
- Celery, cut into strips
- Sautéed shiitake mushrooms
- Stir-fried vegetables
- Sprouts

Pickles

- Ginger pickles
- Cucumber pickles
- Carrot or green bean pickles

Great Combinations

- Sautéed shiitake mushrooms, kale, and toasted sesame seeds
- Steamed carrots, kale, and beets
- Gingered Tempeh and Shiitakes (page 110) with mesclun or Lemony Carrot and Beet Salad (page 111)
- Cucumber, grilled red bell pepper, and avocado
- Spinach and mushrooms
- Sweet potato fries and sautéed shiitake mushrooms

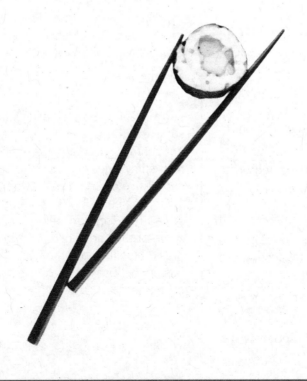

Nori Rolls with Gingered Tofu

In this recipe, grated beets and carrots combine with the tofu, rice, and nori to create a beautiful mosaic pattern in every slice of this delicious nori roll. Once you've tried this version, expand your horizons and use this as a master recipe for making any type of nori rolls you like. The "sushi extravaganza" on pages 106-107 offers lots of suggestions for seasonal vegetables and other fillings you can use. When you mix and match them in combination with the rice recipes on pages 101 through 102, the possibilities are endless—not to mention fun and delicious!

MAKES 8 NORI ROLLS

About 4 cups of cooked rice (see recipes on pages 101 through 104)

1 tablespoon light sesame oil

1 tablespoon tamari

1 tablespoon grated fresh ginger

14 ounces extra-firm tofu, sliced into long rectangles about ½ inch thick

2 cups grated beets

1 cup grated carrots

8 sheets toasted nori

2 to 3 tablespoons umeboshi paste

2 tablespoons wasabi powder, or more as needed

2 tablespoons water

Tamari

Start by cooking the rice as directed in the recipe of your choice. While the rice cools, heat the oil, tamari, and ginger in a medium-size skillet over medium heat. Add the tofu and fry for 3 to 5 minutes on each side, until golden brown on both sides. (You may need to do a couple of rounds of frying to cook all of the tofu. No need to add more oil if you do.) Slice the tofu slabs into thirds the long way to make long strips.

Mix the beets and carrots together in a bowl.

Lay a sushi mat on a clean work surface with the bamboo strips running horizontally. Place a piece of nori on the mat, shiny side down. Spread about ½ cup of rice on the nori, leaving the top 1½ inches bare. Lay 2 or 3 strips of tofu across the rice, horizontally, followed by some of the carrot-beet mixture. Gently press the filling into the rice. Spread some umeboshi paste over the top inch of the nori.

Starting at the end closest to you and using even pressure, use the sushi mat to roll the nori tightly and evenly around the rice and fillings. Be sure to pull the leading edge of the mat back so it doesn't get incorporated into the roll. Once the rolling is completed, give the mat a gentle squeeze along its entire length, then let the nori roll sit inside the mat for a minute to ensure a tight roll. Gently unroll the mat and slice the roll into 8 rounds (for best results, use a very sharp serrated knife). Repeat with the remaining ingredients.

Put the wasabi powder and water in a small bowl and stir to form a paste. For a thinner, less pungent dip, add a little more water.

To serve, place the bowl of wasabi in the center of a platter and surround it with the sushi rounds. Provide small bowls for tamari so that people can mix their wasabi with a bit of tamari if they like.

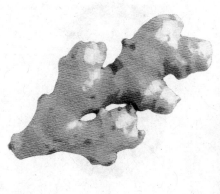

Gingered Tempeh and Shiitakes

Here's another great filling to roll with your choice of rice. Just substitute it for the Gingered Tofu in the master recipe on page 108, using one strip of tempeh per roll. (It doesn't make enough for all eight rolls, but you can mix and match other filling ingredients to make the other two rolls.) And if you like, substitute about 4 ounces of mesclun for the beets and carrots (use a small handful of mesclun for each roll). Most varieties of tempeh are gluten-free, but occasionally you'll come across a multigrain version or another type that contains gluten, so check the label to be sure.

MAKES ENOUGH
FILLING FOR 6
NORI ROLLS

8 ounces tempeh,
cut into 6 long
strips

1 tablespoon
sesame oil

1 tablespoon tamari

2 tablespoons
grated fresh ginger

¾ cup water

4 ounces shiitake
mushrooms,
stemmed and sliced

Heat the oil, tamari, and ginger in a medium-size skillet over medium heat. Add the tempeh and fry for a few minutes, until almost all of the oil is absorbed. Flip the tempeh over, then add the water and mushrooms. Cook for a few minutes longer, until the tempeh absorbs the water. Flip the mushrooms and tempeh over and fry for a minute or two longer, until the tempeh is brown on both sides and the mushrooms are tender.

110

Lemony Carrot and Beet Salad

This light, refreshing salad is wonderful on its own, as a side dish, and equally wonderful rolled into nori rolls with Gingered Tempeh and Shiitakes (page 110). If you're using it as a filling in nori rolls, omit the oil and salt.

MAKES ENOUGH
FILLING FOR 6 TO
8 NORI ROLLS;
SERVES 4 AS A
SIDE SALAD

2 cups grated
carrots

2 cups grated beets

Chopped watercress
or mustard greens
(optional)

¼ cup freshly
squeezed lemon
juice

1 tablespoon
flaxseed oil,
hempseed oil, or
toasted sesame oil

½ teaspoon sea salt

Put all of the ingredients in a medium-sized bowl and mix thoroughly.

Variations

✣ Try different combinations: carrots, beets, and daikon; carrots, daikon, and mustard greens; or carrots and watercress.

✣ Swap 1 to 3 tablespoons rice vinegar for the lemon juice.

✣ Swap 1 to 3 tablespoons umeboshi vinegar for the lemon and omit the salt.

111

Naturally Fermented Pickled Vegetables

These pickles are easy to make and ready in just three or four days. They're also easy to digest, and kids of all ages love them. Use one or more of the vegetables listed, choosing based on what's in season and looks best—and your preferences of course! Once the pickles are ready, try slicing them to use as a filling for nori rolls, or just serve them alongside as an accompaniment.

MAKES 1 GALLON

2 to 3 pounds of pickling cucumbers, carrots, broccoli spears or florets, cauliflower florets, string beans, or a combination

2 dill blossoms or 1 tablespoon dill seed

2 to 4 cloves garlic

1 large red onion, quartered

10 cups water

⅓ cup sea salt

Rinse the vegetables and put them in a large sterile gallon jar or crock. Add the dill, garlic, and onion.

Put the water and salt in large saucepan over high heat. Bring to a boil, then lower the heat and simmer, stirring occasionally, for two to three minutes, until the salt dissolves to make a brine.

Let the mixture cool to room temperature, then pour it over the vegetables. (Some of the vegetables will float.) Put the lid on the jar but don't seal it tightly, or cover the crock with a lid or a plate. Set the pickles in your pantry, a dry basement, or a dark, cool corner of your kitchen counter for 3 or 4 days. If using a jar, cover it with a dish towel to keep it in the dark.

After the 3 or 4 days, taste the pickles. If they are as sour as you like, they're ready to eat. If not, let them sit for another day. If they're too salty, don't worry; you can just rinse them or soak them in cool water for a day before you use them. Stored in an airtight container in the refrigerator, the pickles will keep for 1 month.

CHAPTER 6

super sides

You can put together a very tasty, satisfying, and nutritious meal by serving a variety of side dishes. In fact, with the addition of a sauce or other tasty topping, many side dishes can be instantly transformed into exciting and satisfying entrées.

It's getting to be common knowledge that we can all benefit from eating more whole grains, but for all too many folks, that ends up being translated into endless repetitions of plain brown rice. In recent years, a wide variety of more exotic rices have become available, and I've given you several recipes to entice you into trying some of them, including Jade Pearl Rice with Almonds and Green Beans (page 127) and Madagascar Pink Rice with Cashews and Scallions (page 129). Other grain side dishes in this chapter will guide and inspire you in experimenting with grains other than rice, or combinations of grains, to enliven your plate and your senses. So branch out beyond rice to try Millet and Sweet Carrots (page 123), Quinoa and Shiitake Pilaf (page 124), or Kasha Varnishkes (page 133).

You'll be happy to find Corn Fritters (page 140) and Amaranth and Corn Flatbread (page 141) in these pages. These accompaniments can take the place of bread at any meal, as can Corn Muffins (page 49), from the breakfast chapter. This chapter also includes several hearty salads, such as Mediterranean Rice Salad (page 132) and Salsa Salad with Tomatillos and Pinto Beans (page 136). When the weather is hot, why not lighten things up and make a meal of one or more of these salads, perhaps served atop a bed of baby salad greens? You'll find hearty vegetable dishes that are the perfect antidote to winter's chill, as well, from warming Hearty Greens and Tofu in Tahini Sauce (page 137) to Basmati Soup with Indian Spices (page 142).

The winter holidays can be particularly challenging if you're on a gluten-free diet. It's a time when we typically gather with loved ones to share traditional meals, and quite a few of the time-honored dishes include wheat. Rather than focusing on what you can't have, celebrate what you can have! If you're one of those people who thinks Thanksgiving is all about the side dishes anyway, this chapter offers some wonderful gluten-free dishes that will grace any holiday table. Try Spiced Yams with Pecans (page 139) and Basmati and Wild Rice Pilaf (page 125), accompanied by Cranberry-Cherry Sauce (page 161). Of course you'll want to ladle some Mushroom-Leek Sauce (page 151), from chapter 7, over your mashed potatoes. And if you serve Savory Stuffed Winter Squash (page 72), from chapter 4, as the centerpiece of the meal, I guarantee you won't go away hungry. Just be sure to save some room for Granny Smith Apple Crumb Pie (page 190) or Pear and Cranberry Crisp (page 193), in chapter 8.

Aztec Two-Step

Millet and amaranth make for a tasty duet, and the combination is particularly convenient because they have the same cooking time. Try this simple cooked grain dish topped with Marinated Dried Tomatoes (page 171) or Tomato Sauce with Fennel and Marinated Dried Tomatoes (page 152). Or for a nice light meal that plays on the Aztec theme, serve it alongside Salsa Salad with Tomatillos and Pinto Beans (page 136) or Sweet Potato and Black Bean Chili with Tomatillos (page 88).

SERVES 6 TO 8

6 cups water or vegetable stock

1½ cups millet, rinsed

½ cup amaranth

Pinch of sea salt

Combine all of the ingredients in a large saucepan over high heat. Bring to a boil, then lower the heat, cover, and simmer for 20 to 25 minutes, until all of the water is absorbed.

Variations

❧ For a breakfast dish, add ½ cup of currants, dates, or raisins.

❧ Sauté the grains with 2 cloves of chopped garlic and 1 cup of chopped onion before adding the water and salt.

❧ To use a pressure cooker with a rice crock instead of a saucepan, decrease the amount of water or vegetable stock to 3 cups and cook for about 20 minutes, following the method on page 36.

Sunny Mountain Rice

The sunflower seeds add a nice texture that's both soft and crunchy, and the quinoa lends a flavor reminiscent of sesame seeds. To build a meal around this delicious side dish, serve it alongside Butternut Squash and Tempeh Stew with Shiitake Mushrooms (page 83), Spiced Yams with Pecans (page 139), or Tomato-Lentil Stew with Kale (page 146).

SERVES 6 TO 8

6 cups water

Pinch of sea salt

2 cups brown rice (any variety), rinsed

1 cup quinoa, rinsed

½ cup raw sunflower seeds, presoaked if you like (see page 78)

1 cup chopped parsley or scallions (white and green parts), for garnish

Bring the water and salt to a boil in a large saucepan over high heat. Stir in the rice, quinoa, and sunflower seeds. Lower the heat, cover, and simmer for about 40 minutes, until all of the water is absorbed. Garnish with the parsley or scallions before serving.

Variations

❧ To use a pressure cooker with a rice crock instead of a saucepan, decrease the amount of water or vegetable stock to 3½ cups and cook for about 40 minutes, following the method on page 36.

Power Pilaf with Brown Rice, Quinoa, and Wild Rice

Here's a fantastic trio of tasty grains that offers a complete protein. For a divine meal, serve it with Shiitake Soup with Cashew Cream (page 144), with a dollop of Cranberry-Cherry Sauce (page 161) alongside the pilaf.

SERVES 6 TO 8

5 cups water

Pinch of sea salt

1½ cups short-grain brown rice, rinsed

½ cup quinoa, rinsed

½ cup wild rice

1 bay leaf

Bring the water and salt to a boil in a large saucepan over high heat. Stir in the rice, quinoa, wild rice, and bay leaf. Lower the heat, cover, and simmer for 45 to 60 minutes, until all of the water is absorbed.

Variations

❧ To use a pressure cooker with a rice crock instead of a saucepan, decrease the amount of water to 3 cups and cook for about 45 minutes, following the method on page 36.

Bronze Delight

Kasha is simply toasted buckwheat groats, and you can definitely make your own at home. Just toast the buckwheat groats in a dry pan in a 375°F oven for about 20 minutes, and you're good to go. Like teff, it's a quick-cooking grain, and the two make a tasty combination. Use ivory teff to contrast with the brown kasha, or brown teff to match it. If you let this dish cool after cooking, you can slice it into wedges and serve them smothered with Mushroom-Leek Sauce (page 151) or garnished with chopped parsley or scallions. To round out the meal, try Spiced Yams with Pecans (page 139), Tomato-Lentil Stew with Kale (page 146), or Hearty Greens and Tofu in Tahini Sauce (page 137).

SERVES ABOUT 4

1 cup kasha

½ cup teff

Pinch of sea salt

3½ cups boiling water

Toast the kasha, teff, and salt in a medium-size saucepan over medium-high heat, stirring often, for about 3 minutes, just until the grains are hot and begin to pop. Lower the heat, then slowly pour in the water. Cover and simmer for about 15 minutes, until all of the water is absorbed.

Lemony Quinoa Salad with Toasted Sunflower Seeds

With its bright, sprightly flavors, this is a wonderful springtime dish. But there's nothing to say you can't serve it with a green salad in summer or roasted vegetables in winter. To make the sunflower seeds more easily digestible, soak them overnight beforehand.

SERVES 6 TO 8

3¾ cups water

½ teaspoon sea salt

2½ cups quinoa, rinsed

1 cup raw sunflower seeds, presoaked if you like (see page 78)

¾ cup freshly squeezed lemon juice

¼ cup extra-virgin olive oil

Bring the water and salt to a boil in a medium-size saucepan. Add the quinoa, then lower the heat, cover, and simmer for about 15 minutes, until all of the water is absorbed. Transfer the quinoa to a large bowl and let it cool to room temperature.

Meanwhile, toast the sunflower seeds in a dry skillet over medium heat, stirring often, for 3 to 5 minutes, until they are aromatic and start to pop. Add the sunflower seeds to the quinoa, along with the lemon juice and oil, and stir until well combined. Taste and adjust the seasonings if desired.

Variations

◈ Swap pumpkin seeds for the sunflower seeds.

◈ Forgo toasting the sunflower seeds; instead, add them to the saucepan when you add the quinoa.

Quinoa with Herbs and Toasted Sunflower Seeds: Increase the amount of sunflower seeds to 1¼ cups. Omit the lemon juice and increase the amount of olive oil to 7 tablespoons. Add ½ cup of chopped marjoram or oregano leaves when you stir everything together. Taste and adjust the seasonings; you may want more salt.

Quinoa Tabouli: Add 1 cup of chopped parsley and 1 cup of chopped scallions when you stir everything together.

Black Forbidden Rice
with Sunflower Seeds

The color contrast between the black forbidden rice and pale sunflower seeds makes this easy and very tasty side dish visually stunning. If you don't have black forbidden rice on hand, you can certainly use other varieties, such as long-grain brown rice, basmati rice, or jasmine rice, adjusting the cooking time as indicated in chapter 2. To make the sunflower seeds more easily digestible, soak them overnight beforehand.

SERVES 6 TO 8

5 cups water

2½ cups black forbidden rice

1 cup raw sunflower seeds, presoaked if you like (see page 78)

Pinch of sea salt

Combine all of the ingredients in a large saucepan over high heat. Bring to a boil, then lower the heat, cover, and simmer for about 30 minutes, until all of the water is absorbed.

Variations

◄ Swap pumpkin seeds for the sunflower seeds.

Millet and Sweet Carrots

In this gorgeous golden dish, naturally sweet-flavored millet is paired with carrots, but you could also use delicata or butternut squash to create a similar effect. If you like, you can substitute other vegetables for some of the carrots. Leeks or cauliflower florets would be good choices.

SERVES 4 TO 6

4½ cups water

1½ cups millet, rinsed

3 large carrots, sliced

1 cup coarsely chopped onion

Pinch of sea salt

Combine all of the ingredients in a large saucepan over high heat. Bring to a boil, then lower the heat, cover, and simmer for 20 to 25 minutes, until all of the liquid is absorbed.

Variations

⚜ To use a pressure cooker with a rice crock instead of a saucepan, decrease the amount of water or vegetable stock to 3 cups and cook for about 20 minutes, following the method on page 36.

⚜ **Millet Croquettes:** When the cooked millet is cool enough to handle, shape it into balls or patties and fry or deep-fry them.

⚜ **Millet Veggie Loaf:** Transfer the hot millet to an unoiled standard loaf pan. When it cools, slice and serve topped with Creamy Cilantro Sauce with Ginger (page 159) or Mushroom-Leek Sauce (page 151).

Quinoa and Shiitake Pilaf

Leeks, celery, and mushrooms enliven this pilaf and give it a flavor reminiscent of a Thanksgiving stuffing. If you like, you can substitute other types of mushrooms for the shiitakes. White button mushrooms, criminis, or portobellos would all be great choices.

SERVES 6 TO 8

1½ tablespoons extra-virgin olive oil

2½ cups chopped leeks (white and tender green parts)

2 cups chopped celery

1½ cups stemmed and sliced shiitake mushrooms

1¾ cups quinoa, rinsed

½ teaspoon sea salt

3½ cups boiling water

Heat the oil in a medium-size saucepan or skillet (one with a tight-fitting lid) over medium heat. Add the leeks, celery, and mushrooms and sauté, stirring continuously for about 5 minutes, until the vegetables become fragrant and their colors brighten. Stir in the quinoa and salt. Lower the heat, then slowly pour in the water. Cover and simmer for about 15 minutes, until all of the water is absorbed.

Basmati and Wild Rice Pilaf

This festive savory pilaf is perfect for Thanksgiving and other winter holidays. For a winning combination, serve it with Butternut Squash and Tempeh Stew with Shiitake Mushrooms (page 83) and a dollop of Cranberry-Cherry Sauce (page 161).

SERVES ABOUT 8

2 cups brown basmati rice

1 cup wild rice

⅔ cup chopped walnuts, presoaked if you like (see page 78)

1 teaspoon sea salt

1 tablespoon extra-virgin olive oil

1½ cups sliced celery

1 cup sliced onion or leek (white and tender green parts)

6 cups boiling water

1 teaspoon dried thyme, or 1 tablespoon fresh thyme

1 cup sliced scallions (white and green parts), for garnish

Toast the basmati, wild rice, walnuts, and salt in a large saucepan over medium-high heat, stirring continuously, for 3 to 5 minutes, until the grains start to pop and have a nutty aroma. Add the oil, celery, and onion and sauté for about 5 minutes, until the onion softens and the celery is bright green. Lower the heat, then slowly pour in the water. Cover and simmer for about 40 minutes, until all of the water is absorbed. Stir in the thyme. Taste and adjust the seasonings if desired. Garnish with the scallions before serving.

Wild Rice and Cranberry Pilaf

If you're craving holiday fare but don't want to spend all day in the kitchen, consider this festive pilaf. It's quick and easy to put together, and the combination of sautéed aromatic vegetables, wild rice, and cranberries will hit the spot.

SERVES ABOUT 4

2 tablespoons extra-virgin olive oil

1½ cups wild rice

3 cups coarsely chopped leeks (white and tender green parts)

1½ cups sliced celery

½ cup sliced red bell pepper

1½ teaspoon sea salt

4½ cups boiling water

½ cup cranberries

Heat the oil in a large saucepan over medium heat. Add the wild rice, leeks, celery, bell pepper, and salt and sauté for about 5 minutes, until the vegetables take on a brighter hue. Lower the heat, then slowly pour in the water. Add the cranberries. Cover and simmer for 30 to 40 minutes, until all of the water is absorbed.

Jade Pearl Rice with Almonds and Green Beans

With green beans to complement the jade-colored rice and red onions for contrast, this is a beautiful dish—and delicious too. Sautéing the rice gives it a wonderfully rich flavor, and almonds add a nice crunch. If you can't track down any Jade Pearl rice, it's fine to substitute other varieties, such as long-grain brown, basmati, or black forbidden rice. If you like, soak the almonds overnight to make them easier to digest.

SERVES 4 TO 6

1 tablespoon sesame oil

½ cup chopped red onion

1 cup cut green beans, in bite-size pieces

⅔ cup raw almonds, presoaked if you like (see page 78)

2 cups Jade Pearl rice

1 teaspoon sea salt

4 cups boiling water

2 bay leaves

Heat the oil in a large saucepan over medium heat. Add the onion and sauté for about 3 minutes, until it takes on a brighter hue. Add the green beans, almonds, rice, and salt and cook, stirring constantly, for 3 minutes. Lower the heat, then slowly pour in the water. Add the bay leaves. Cover and simmer for about 15 minutes, until all of the water is absorbed.

Coconut Jasmine Rice with Goji Berries and Shiitakes

If you serve this sweet and satisfying pilaf topped with Creamy Cilantro Sauce with Ginger (page 159), it could definitely take center stage. Celtic Sea Salt is especially good in this dish, but regular sea salt will do. Goji berries are so healthful that they're well worth seeking out, but if you don't have any on hand, you could also make this with dried cranberries.

SERVES ABOUT 4

2 cups water

Pinch of sea salt

1 cup brown
jasmine rice

⅓ cup dried shiitake
mushrooms,
stemmed and
broken into pieces

⅓ cup unsweetened
shredded coconut

2 tablespoons goji
berries

Put the water and salt in a medium-size saucepan over high heat. Bring to a boil, then stir in the rice, shiitakes, coconut, and goji berries. Lower the heat, cover, and simmer for 30 to 40 minutes, until all of the water is absorbed.

Variations

◈ If you don't have goji berries, you could try currants or dried cranberries—or just leave them out.

Madagascar Pink Rice with Cashews and Scallions

For a great summer meal, serve this cumin- and ginger-scented rice alongside a bean salad. Madagascar pink rice has an enticing color and an unusual, almost tropical flavor, but if you can't find it, basmati or brown rice would also work well. If you do have access to some of the newer, more exotic varieties of rice, you might also try this with Bhutanese red rice, which will imbue the dish with a deep russet red color. If you use Bhutanese red rice, increase the cooking time to about 20 minutes; for basmati or brown rice, increase to about 40 minutes.

SERVES ABOUT 4

1 tablespoon ghee (see page 86) or extra-virgin coconut oil

1 teaspoon cumin seeds

1 cup Madagascar pink rice

½ cup raw cashews

2 cups boiling water

1 teaspoon grated fresh ginger

½ teaspoon sea salt

½ cup chopped scallions (white and green parts), for garnish

Heat the ghee in a medium-size saucepan over medium heat. Add the cumin and cook, stirring, for 1 to 2 minutes, until the seeds smell fragrant. Add the rice and cashews and sauté for about 2 minutes. Lower the heat, then slowly pour in the water. Add the ginger and salt. Cover and simmer for 15 to 20 minutes, until all of the water is absorbed. Garnish with the scallions before serving.

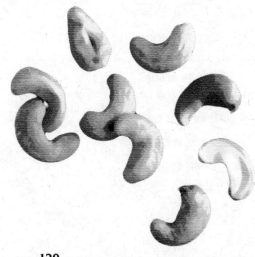

Bhutanese Red Rice Pilaf
with Vegetables

This dish is a good example of how you can mix and match not just ingredients, but also cooking methods. Although the method is similar to a pilaf, I start by stir-frying ingredients with an Asian flair, including a generous amount of fresh vegetables. The result is extremely flavorful and colorful, and not unlike fried rice. Bhutanese red rice imparts another layer of color to the dish, but if don't have any on hand, you could also use brown rice; brown basmati or brown jasmine rice would be especially good choices. For any type of brown rice, increase the cooking time to about 40 minutes.

SERVES 6 TO 8

3 tablespoons sesame oil

1 tablespoon grated fresh ginger

4 cloves garlic, minced or pressed

1 teaspoon dried chile flakes

1 cup sliced daikon

1 cup diagonally sliced celery

¾ cup julienned carrots

2 cups Bhutanese red rice

4 cups boiling water

1 tablespoon tamari

1 cup chopped scallions (white and green parts)

Heat a wok or large skillet (one with a tight-fitting lid) over high heat. Add the oil, ginger, garlic, and chile flakes and stir-fry for about 1 minute, until fragrant. Add the daikon, celery, and carrots and stir-fry for 2 to 3 minutes to infuse the vegetables with flavor. Add the rice and stir-fry for 2 minutes. Lower the heat, then slowly, pour in the water. Add the tamari. Cover and simmer for about 20 minutes, until the water is absorbed. Stir in the scallions or use them as a garnish. Taste and adjust the seasonings if desired.

Sorghum with Summer Squash and Red Bell Peppers

Sorghum has a light nutty, flavor and has a nicely chewy texture. The first time I tried it was in a delicious lemony marinated salad with fresh mint. As I researched other ways to cook it, I discovered that it is also pairs well with onions and garlic. Here, I've added summer squash and red bell pepper for a beautiful and tasty side dish. I recommend that you soak the sorghum overnight, to make it more tender and easily digestible once it's cooked, so plan ahead.

SERVES ABOUT 4

1 tablespoon sesame oil or ghee (see page 86)

1 cup chopped red onion

2 cloves garlic, sliced

1 tablespoon grated fresh ginger

1 cup sorghum, soaked at least 6 hours, rinsed, and drained

1 teaspoon sea salt

1 teaspoon ground fenugreek seeds

3 cups boiling water

1 cup sliced summer squash, in half-moons

⅔ cup julienned red bell pepper

½ cup sliced carrot, in half-moons

1 cup chopped cilantro

Heat the oil in a large saucepan over medium heat. Add the onion, garlic, and ginger and sauté for about 5 minutes, until the onion softens. Stir in the sorghum and sauté for 3 to 5 minutes to infuse it with flavor. Stir in the salt and fenugreek. Lower the heat, then slowly pour in the water. Cover and simmer for 30 to 40 minutes, until most of the water is absorbed.

Add the squash, bell pepper, and carrot. Continue simmering for about 15 minutes, until all of the water is absorbed and the sorghum is tender. Stir everything together, then taste and adjust the seasonings if desired. Stir in the cilantro or use it as a garnish.

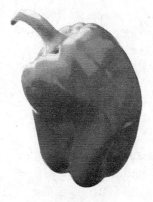

Mediterranean Rice Salad

Mint, oregano, olives, and capers combine to create a fabulous and festive rice salad that's perfect summertime fare, especially when served alongside Mediterranean White Bean Salad with Pine Nuts and Capers (page 135). If you don't have homemade Marinated Dried Tomatoes (page 171) on hand, it's fine to use store-bought. This is a great dish to make with leftover cooked rice, but you can also start by cooking the rice from scratch, using 1⅓ cups rice, 2⅔ cups water, and a pinch of sea salt (see page 27 for the method). Be sure to cool the rice to room temperature before mixing up the salad, or the mint and oregano will wilt.

SERVES 4 TO 6

4 cups cooked long-grain brown rice, brown basmati, or a combination of the two, at room temperature

½ cup fresh mint leaves, chopped

½ cup fresh oregano leaves, chopped

1 cup sliced red onion

Juice of 1 lemon

5 Marinated Dried Tomatoes (page 171), sliced

2 tablespoons of marinade from the Marinated Dried Tomatoes

¼ cup pitted kalamata olives

¼ cup capers, rinsed

1 zucchini, quartered lengthwise and sliced

Put all of the ingredients in a bowl and stir until thoroughly combined. Taste and adjust the seasonings if desired.

Kasha Varnishkes

When I was growing up, the only whole grain my mother made was kasha, and she made it so well that I still consult her. Here's a gluten-free variation of her kasha varnishkes, made with golden quinoa-corn elbows. Corn pasta provides great eye appeal, but you can use any type of gluten-free shaped pasta. Kasha is simply toasted buckwheat groats, so if you like, you can make your own. Just toast the buckwheat groats in a dry pan in a 375°F oven for about 20 minutes, and you're good to go. For a warming meal on a cold winter night, serve this dish alongside Hearty Greens and Tofu in Tahini Sauce (page 137).

SERVES 6 TO 8

1½ cups quinoa-corn elbows

2 tablespoons extra-virgin olive oil

1 large onion, chopped

Sea salt

⅓ cup raw sunflower seeds, presoaked if you like (see page 78)

1⅓ cups kasha

2⅔ cups boiling water

1 cup chopped parsley

Cook the pasta in a generous amount of boiling water until just tender. Drain and rinse in cold water.

Meanwhile, heat the oil in a large saucepan over medium heat, add the onions and a pinch of salt, and sauté for about 5 minutes, until the onion begins to soften.

Toast the sunflower seeds in a dry medium-size skillet over medium heat, stirring often, for 3 to 5 minutes, until they are aromatic and start to pop. Add the kasha and ½ teaspoon of salt and toast for about 1 minute to warm the kasha. (This will make it turn out lighter and fluffier.)

Stir the kasha and toasted sunflower seeds into the sautéed onions. Lower the heat, then slowly pour in the water. Cover and simmer for 10 to 15 minutes, until all of the water is absorbed.

Fluff the kasha with a fork, then add the pasta and chopped parsley and stir gently until evenly incorporated. Serve immediately.

Warm Soba Salad with Arame and Beets

Steamed beets lend sweetness to this tasty Asian salad, parsley and scallions add color and zest, and arame, a black, delicate, mineral-rich sea vegetable, contributes a slightly sweet taste and a texture like angel hair pasta. Remember, black goes with everything, so feel free to use whatever vegetables are in season and look appealing; carrots, radishes, or red or green cabbage would all be great choices. It's important to cut the beets into large pieces, or they could fall through some steamer baskets. You could also cut them in half-moons.

SERVES ABOUT 4

2 cups diced beets, in large cubes

4 ounces 100% buckwheat soba noodles

½ cup arame

2 cups chopped parsley

¾ cup chopped scallions (white and green parts)

1½ tablespoons sesame oil or toasted sesame oil

2½ tablespoons umeboshi vinegar or tamari

2 tablespoons rice vinegar

Steam the beets for 15 to 20 minutes, until tender to your liking. Save ½ cup of the steaming water.

Meanwhile, cook the noodles in a generous amount of boiling water until al dente. Drain, rinse in cold water, then set aside to drain.

Put the arame in a large mixing bowl. Pour the ½ cup of water from steaming the beets over the arame to rehydrate it, and put the beets on top. Let stand for about 5 minutes, until the arame softens.

Add the parsley, scallions, sesame oil, umeboshi vinegar, and rice vinegar and stir until well combined. Gently stir in the soba. Taste and adjust the seasonings if desired. Serve immediately as a warm salad, or at room temperature or even chilled.

Mediterranean White Bean Salad with Pine Nuts and Capers

Made with summer-sweet vegetables, fresh dill, and cooked beans, this main dish salad is an excellent warm-weather lunch. Bring along some Vegetarian Sushi from chapter 5 for great picnic. Enjoy!

SERVES 4 TO 6

3 cups cooked navy beans (see page 80)

5 cups thinly sliced red cabbage

1 cup chopped scallions (white and green parts)

1 cup minced fresh dill

¾ cup freshly squeezed lemon juice

¼ cup extra-virgin olive oil

⅔ cup pine nuts, presoaked if you like (see page 78)

½ cup capers, rinsed

Put all of the ingredients in a large bowl and stir until well combined. Taste and adjust the seasonings if desired.

Variations

◄ You can substitute other cooked beans; try chickpeas, cannellini beans, or, for a twist on the Mediterranean theme, pinto beans.

135

Salsa Salad with Tomatillos and Pinto Beans

As the end of summer approaches, take advantage of the bounty of tomatillos, juicy tomatoes, and peppers to make this colorful and fresh-tasting salad. Yellow tomatoes will add to the eye appeal, but you can use any type of heirloom or cherry tomatoes (except plum tomatoes) as long at they're vine ripe and flavorful. To transform this salad into a main dish, scoop it up with quesadillas made with corn tortillas.

SERVES 4 TO 6

3 cups quartered tomatillos

1½ cups cooked pinto beans (see page 80)

1½ cups chopped yellow tomatoes

1 cup diced red bell pepper

1 cup chopped cilantro

½ cup diced red onion

5 tablespoons freshly squeezed lime juice

2 cloves garlic, pressed

½ teaspoon sea salt

Put all of the ingredients in a large bowl and stir gently until well combined. Taste and adjust the seasonings if desired.

Variations

❧ Swap other cooked beans, such as kidney or black beans, for the pinto beans.

Hearty Greens and Tofu in Tahini Sauce

Think creamed spinach, but heartier and higher in calcium, without a speck of dairy. Serve with Kasha Varnishkes (page 133) or simply beside or on top of cooked kasha.

SERVES 4 TO 6

2 tablespoons extra-virgin olive oil

1½ cups chopped red onions or leeks (white and tender green parts)

6 cloves garlic, sliced, or 6 garlic scapes, sliced

3 tablespoons umeboshi vinegar

3 cups chopped broccoli

4 cups tightly packed chopped kale, in bite-size pieces

1 cup water

1 pound extra-firm tofu, cut into bite-size cubes

⅓ cup tahini

Heat the oil in a wok or large skillet over medium-high heat. Add the onions, garlic, and umeboshi vinegar and sauté for about 1 minute. Add the broccoli and sauté for about 3 minutes, until bright green. Add the kale and water and simmer, stirring often, for about 5 minutes, or until the kale is tender to your liking. Gently stir in the tofu.

Push tofu and vegetables off to the side of the wok. Add the tahini and mix it into the liquid in the pan until it forms a creamy sauce. Gently stir the vegetables and tofu into the sauce. Taste and adjust the seasonings if desired; you may want to add more umeboshi vinegar for a tangy, saltier flavor. For a creamier consistency, add more tahini and water.

Variations

❧ Feel free to swap collard greens, chard, or beet greens for the kale. Or use just one green vegetable rather than two: broccoli, kale, or collard greens.

❧ Swap a sliced zucchini or other summer squash for the tofu.

Garlicky Baked Beans with Parsnips and Butternut Squash

In this warming dish, the beans are combined with winter vegetables and baked for a generous amount of time, until deliciously infused with garlic and rosemary. For a great meal, serve this dish with your favorite winter grain, such as kasha, and garnish with chèvre, if you like.

SERVES 4 TO 6

2¼ cups cooked pinto beans (see page 80)

2 cups cubed butternut squash

2 cups sliced parsnips

1 head of garlic, peeled and coarsely chopped

2½ tablespoons extra-virgin olive oil

1½ teaspoons minced fresh rosemary

1½ teaspoons sea salt

Preheat the oven to 400°F.

Put all of the ingredients in a baking dish and stir until thoroughly combined. Cover and bake for about 1 hour, until the squash is tender. Taste and adjust the seasonings if desired. Serve immediately.

Variation

⚜ Swap other winter root vegetables, such as celeriac, carrots, or potatoes, for all or some of the parsnips.

Spiced Yams with Pecans

Here's a warming winter dish that's perfect for the winter holidays. I've included a bit of butter here for its rich flavor, but if you'd like to make a vegan version, you could certainly replace it with another tablespoon of canola or coconut oil.

SERVES 6 TO 8

8 cups diced yams, cut into 1-inch cubes

½ cup pecan halves

2 tablespoons canola oil or melted extra-virgin coconut oil

3 tablespoons maple syrup

1 tablespoon unsalted butter, cut into small pieces

1½ teaspoons ground cinnamon

1¼ teaspoons ground nutmeg, preferably freshly grated

½ teaspoon sea salt

Preheat the oven to 400°F.

Combine all of the ingredients in a baking dish and toss until the yams are evenly coated. Cover and bake for 50 to 60 minutes, until the yams are tender. Taste and adjust the seasonings if desired. Serve immediately.

Variation

❧ Swap walnuts for the pecans, or omit the nuts altogether.

Corn Fritters

When my kids were little, they loved this dish so much that I made it at least once a week. Now that they're grown, they still love it. Bean dishes and steamed vegetables both complement these fritters; serve all three together for a simple and satisfying meal. The method here involves first cooking the teff and cornmeal, then letting them cool for at least an hour to set up, so plan ahead.

SERVES ABOUT 4

1 cup cornmeal

⅓ cup teff

4 cups boiling water

Pinch of sea salt

3 tablespoons extra-virgin olive oil

3 tablespoons tamari

Toast the cornmeal and teff in a large dry skillet over medium heat for about 5 minutes, until the grains develop a nutty aroma. Lower the heat, then slowly pour in the water. Add the salt. Simmer, stirring occasionally to prevent lumps, for 10 to 20 minutes, until all of the water is absorbed. Turn off the heat and, if necessary, spread the cooked grains in an even layer in the bottom of the skillet. Let the cooked grains cool for at least 1 hour.

When you're ready to cook the fritters, use a spatula to cut the cooked grains into triangles or other shapes. Heat a large, clean skillet over medium-high heat. Add the oil and tamari and swirl to combine, then add a few fritters—however many you can fit while leaving a bit of space between them. Fry the fritters for about 3 to 5 minutes on each side, until golden brown. Serve immediately, or transfer the fritters to a covered dish in a 250°F oven to keep them warm until serving.

Amaranth and Corn Flatbread

Not only is this flatbread easy to make, it's delicious too, especially when cooked in ghee. It's a great accompaniment for just about any soup or stew. I especially like it with Salsa Salad with Tomatillos and Pinto Beans (page 136) or Sweet Potato and Black Bean Chili with Tomatillos (page 88). Because it's so festive and colorful, it also makes a great appetizer.

SERVES 3 OR 4

1 cup amaranth flour

½ cup corn flour

1 teaspoon sea salt

½ cup lukewarm water

⅓ cup minced onion

½ cup minced red or green bell pepper

2 to 3 tablespoons ghee (see page 86) or sesame oil

½ cup grated Cheddar cheese (about 2 ounces; optional)

Coat a work surface with ¼ cup amaranth flour or corn flour.

Combine the amaranth flour, corn flour, salt, and water in a bowl. Mix until the dough comes together, then add the onion and bell pepper and mix them in. Transfer the dough to the work surface and knead for a few minutes, until slightly sticky. Use your hands to shape dough into flat rounds about 2 or 3 inches in diameter.

Put the ghee in a small skillet over medium-high heat. Once it melts, swirl it around to coat the pan. Fry the flatbreads for about 3 minutes on each side, until browned and crisp. Sprinkle a bit of cheese atop each flatbread and let it melt, if you like. Serve warm.

Variation

◆ Add a few tablespoons of cooked corn kernels for a colorful and tasty variation.

Basmati Soup with Indian Spices

In this sweet and nourishing fall soup, cinnamon, ginger, cumin, mustard, garlic, and fennel warm you from the inside and offer immune support, to help you avoid all of the ailments cold weather can bring. The ghee fits the theme and lends a rich, satisfying flavor, but if you'd like to make a vegan version, just substitute extra-virgin coconut oil, extra-virgin olive oil, sesame oil, or sunflower oil.

Variations

- For a lighter soup, toast the cumin, fennel, and mustard seeds in a dry skillet, without oil or ghee.

- For a spicier soup, add some cayenne pepper when you add the rice.

- You can use a large pressure cooker instead of a soup pot. After you add the boiling water, lock on the pressure cooker lid. Bring the pot to pressure over high heat. After 2 minutes, adjust the heat to maintain high pressure and cook for 30 minutes. Turn off the heat and let the pressure come down naturally. Taste the rice, and if you'd like it softer, bring the pot back up to pressure and cook about 5 minutes longer.

SERVES 4 TO 6

2 tablespoons ghee
(see page 86)

1 tablespoon cumin
seeds

2 teaspoons fennel
seeds

½ teaspoon
mustard seeds

1 cup brown
basmati rice

1½ cups cubed
delicata squash

2 cloves garlic,
sliced

1 teaspoon sea salt

1 teaspoon ground
cinnamon

¼ teaspoon
turmeric

Pinch of saffron

8 cups boiling water

½ cup coarsely
chopped cilantro

2 tablespoons
grated fresh ginger

Melt the ghee in a soup pot over medium heat. Add the cumin seeds, fennel seeds, and mustard seeds. Cover and fry, stirring occasionally, for about 3 minutes, until you hear the seeds pop. Add the rice, squash, garlic, salt, cinnamon, turmeric, and saffron and sauté for about 5 minutes, until the rice is fragrant. Lower the heat, then slowly pour in the water. Cover and simmer for 40 minutes.

Taste the rice for doneness. If you'd like it more tender, just keep cooking until it's as soft as you like. Stir in the cilantro and ginger. Taste and adjust the seasonings if desired.

Shiitake Soup with Cashew Cream

Cashew butter makes this soup rich and creamy without a drop of dairy, and the shiitakes are very healthful. In China, they've been used for their immune-boosting properties for thousands of years. What a delicious way to ward off colds and flus! When cooking with any type of fresh mushrooms, sauté them first to seal in their flavor, or they will give it all to the broth. For a great meal, serve this heavenly soup with Kasha Varnishkes (page 133) or Amaranth and Corn Flatbread (page 141). Sip on a glass of Merlot and enjoy!

SERVES 6 TO 8

3 tablespoons sunflower oil

3 cups grated yams

3 cups sliced onions, in half-moons

6 cups stemmed and coarsely chopped shiitake mushrooms

1 cup cashew butter (see page 24)

7 cups hot water

1½ cups diced red bell pepper

8 cloves garlic, pressed

1 tablespoon sea salt

Heat the oil in a large soup pot over medium heat. Add the yams and sauté for about 10 minutes, stirring frequently to prevent the yams from sticking. (If they do stick, add just a bit of water.) When yams begin to soften and take on a brighter orange hue, add the onions and sauté for about 30 minutes, until the yams are tender. Add the shiitakes and sauté for about 5 minutes, until the mushrooms begin to soften.

Use a handheld blender to blend the cashew butter and hot water until smooth, then add the mixture to the soup. If you only have a standard blender, put ½ cup of the cashew butter in the blender, add 3½ cups of the hot water, and blend until smooth. The hot liquid can cause the blender lid to pop off, so put the lid on only loosely (so steam can escape), and cover it with a kitchen towel. Add the mixture to the soup and repeat with the remaining cashew butter and water.

Bring the soup to a boil, then lower the heat and simmer for 5 minutes to blend the flavors. Stir in the bell pepper, garlic, and salt.

Variations

❧ Add freshly squeezed lime juice as a final seasoning, or serve the soup with wedges of lime.

❧ Add ground cardamom, preferably freshly ground.

❧ Add the red peppers with the mushrooms to blend the flavors and soften the peppers.

Tomato-Lentil Stew with Kale

This gorgeous and delicious dish is dedicated to my dear friends Mark and Alisa, who love good food—and who don't eat garlic and onions. Serve it with Amaranth and Corn Flatbread (page 141), Corn Fritters (page 140), or Corn Muffins (page 49). Or, for a heartier meal, serve it alongside Sunny Mountain Rice (page 116), Millet and Sweet Carrots (page 123), or any of the simple grain dishes in this chapter, or with your favorite pasta with pesto (see pages 156, 157, and 158 for recipes).

SERVES 4 TO 6

3 tablespoons extra-virgin olive oil

2 tablespoons fennel seeds

1 cup brown lentils, rinsed

4½ cups water

3½ cups diced tomatoes

4 cups tightly packed chopped kale

1 teaspoon dried basil

1 teaspoon sea salt

Heat the oil in a soup pot over medium heat. Add the fennel seeds and cook, stirring occasionally, for 2 to 3 minutes, until fragrant. Add the lentils and cook and stir for 2 minutes to blend the flavors. Pour in the water and bring to a boil. Lower the heat, cover, and simmer for 15 to 20 minutes, until the lentils are soft.

Add the tomatoes and kale. Simmer for 5 to 10 minutes, until the kale is tender to your liking. Stir in the basil and salt. Taste and adjust the seasonings if desired.

CHAPTER 7

savory sauces and tempting toppings

If you're just getting started with green and gluten-free cooking, it may seem challenging at times. Between the seeming restrictions of a gluten-free diet and a perhaps daunting array of new and unusual ingredients, you could feel a bit overwhelmed. The recipes in this chapter will come to your rescue, helping you turn simple cooked grains and vegetables into special, irresistible meals. Toppings can play many roles, adding texture, flavor, balance, or visual beauty—or all of the above! They may be as simple and light as edible flowers or a sprig of parsley or cilantro, or as hearty and warming as a rich, creamy sauce.

In this chapter, you'll find everything from salad dressings to pestos to tomato sauces, and more. To make the most of these sauces and toppings in gluten-free cooking, think outside the box. Sure, pestos and tomato sauces are typically served on pasta. You can certainly use them in that way on gluten-free pastas, and I encourage you to let them entice you to experiment with the wide array of gluten-free pastas now available (see page 154). But consider taking your experimentation a step further to try new combinations. Why not ladle Tomato Sauce with Fennel and Marinated Dried Tomatoes (page 152) over cooked grains, or toss roasted or steamed vegetables with a dollop of Vegan Basil-Walnut Pesto (page 156)?

In these pages you'll also find two wonderfully aromatic Asian-inspired sauces: Creamy Cilantro Sauce with Ginger (page 159) and Thai Peanut Sauce (page 160). Both are perfect for tossing with gluten-free Asian pastas or drizzling over a stir-fry. I've also included a number of salad dressing recipes. I know you'll enjoy them on green salads, but I hope you'll also engage your imagination and your senses and use them to concoct your own main-dish salads. For example, you can use Italian Dressing (page 169) to make a hearty main dish salad by tossing it with bite-size pieces of crisp-tender vegetables and warm, cooked grains or beans—or both. Or transform cooked quinoa into a dish with Southwestern flair by adding chopped green chiles, tomatoes, corn kernels, and cooked black beans and mixing it all together with some Avocado Dressing with Garlic Scapes (page 163).

All of the recipes in this chapter are terrific on pasta, whole grains, and vegetables. So check out what's in season at the market, choose your favorite grains, and experiment to your heart's content. The possibilities are endless.

Great Garnishes

Beyond adding to the eye appeal of a dish, garnishes can enhance flavor, add texture, and even add protein or other nutrients. Here are some garnishes I recommend for grains and pasta dishes. Use just one, or go wild and add several:

- Herbs (sprigs, leaves, or minced): basil, mint, parsley, cilantro, rosemary, thyme, oregano, dill, sage, or whatever you like
- Aromatic vegetables: chopped scallions or chives
- Sprouts: sunflower, pea, chickpea, mung bean, alfalfa, broccoli, radish, and more
- Spices: a sprinkling of paprika, freshly ground black pepper, and so on
- Shredded vegetables: carrots, beets, daikon, and others
- Chopped vegetables: anything crisp and colorful, such as bell peppers in a rainbow of hues
- Sea vegetable (flakes, powder, or strips): kelp, dulse, and toasted nori, among others
- Cheese (preferably local, organic, and grass-fed): chèvre, other goat's milk cheeses, feta, sheep's milk cheeses, and grated flavorful cheeses such as Cheddar, and Parmesan
- Aromatic oils: extra-virgin olive oil, hot chili oil, toasted sesame oil, hempseed oil, and flavored oils
- Edible flowers (be sure you can identify them, as not all flowers are safe to eat): bee balm, calendula, chive flowers, nasturtium, violets, and others
- Soy foods: cubed pan-fried tempeh or baked or deep-fried tofu
- Raw or roasted nuts: pine nuts, cashews, almonds, peanuts, pecans, walnuts, hazelnuts, and more
- Raw or roasted seeds: sesame, sunflower, pumpkin, chia, or hemp, or ground flaxseeds
- Sesame salt (gomasio)
- Marinated Dried Tomatoes (page 171)

Red Wine and Porcini Sauce

Between the porcinis and the red wine, this luscious sauce adds a gourmet touch to any meal. It complements the Red Lentil and Teff Loaf (page 77) beautifully, but it's also perfectly at home atop humbler fare, such as mashed potatoes, steamed greens, or plain cooked grains.

MAKES ABOUT 2½ CUPS

½ cup dried porcini mushrooms

1 cup red wine

2 cups water

2 tablespoons chopped fresh marjoram

1 tablespoon chopped fresh rosemary

2 teaspoons fresh thyme leaves

2 teaspoons sea salt

½ teaspoon pepper

2 tablespoons arrowroot or kudzu powder

¼ cup cold water

Soak the porcinis in the wine for 20 to 30 minutes, until they soften.

Drain the mushrooms, pouring the wine through a coffee filter set over a bowl so you can save the wine to use in the sauce. Chop the mushrooms and put them in a small saucepan, along with the wine and the 2 cups of water. Bring to a boil over medium-high heat, then lower the heat to medium and stir in the marjoram, rosemary, thyme, salt, and pepper.

Dissolve the arrowroot powder in the ¼ cup of cold water. Stir the slurry into the pot and continue cooking and stirring for about 1 minute, until the sauce thickens. Taste and adjust the seasonings if desired.

Mushroom-Leek Sauce

This sauce is delicious over Millet Croquettes (see page 123) and also makes a nice topping for pasta, rice, or baked vegetables. Or try it as a gravy over mashed potatoes. You can make numerous variations by using different herbs. Here, I've used sage and rosemary. Rosemary and thyme makes a great combination for Thanksgiving and other holiday meals.

**MAKES ABOUT
3 CUPS**

3 cups sliced
criminis or white
button mushrooms

1½ cups chopped
leeks (white and
tender green parts)
or onion

1½ cups water

1 teaspoon sea salt

1 teaspoon dried
sage

½ teaspoon fresh
rosemary leaves

¼ teaspoon pepper

2 tablespoons
arrowroot or kudzu
powder

3 tablespoons cold
water

Put the mushrooms, leeks, and the 1½ cups of water in a medium-size saucepan and simmer for about 10 minutes, until the aroma of mushrooms fills the air. Stir in the salt, sage, rosemary, and pepper.

Dissolve the arrowroot powder in the 3 tablespoons of cold water. Stir the slurry into the pot and continue cooking and stirring for about 1 minute, until the sauce thickens. Add salt to taste, then taste again and adjust the other seasonings if desired.

Tomato Sauce with Fennel and Marinated Dried Tomatoes

This is the ultimate pasta sauce to make use of summer's bounty. It makes a lot, so you might want to enjoy some right away and store the rest in the freezer for a taste of sunshine in the middle of winter. It's especially delicious with homemade Marinated Dried Tomatoes (page 171), but store-bought will do in a pinch. When you chop the fennel, taste a bit of the stems; if they're tender, you can use them too. Try this sauce on any gluten-free pasta; brown rice spirals and rigatoni are especially fun shapes.

MAKES ABOUT 8 CUPS

---

2 tablespoons extra-virgin olive oil

½ cup coarsely chopped onion

12 cups coarsely chopped plum tomatoes

½ cup chopped fresh fennel

¼ cup Marinated Dried Tomatoes (page 171)

2 cups fresh basil leaves, chopped

3 tablespoons fresh thyme leaves

3 tablespoons fresh oregano or marjoram

2 teaspoons sea salt

10 cloves garlic, pressed

Heat the oil in a soup pot over medium heat. Add the onion and sauté for about 5 minutes, until it begins to soften. Stir in the tomatoes, fennel, and dried tomatoes and cook, stirring occasionally, until hot and bubbling. Lower the heat, cover, and simmer, stirring occasionally, for an hour or two, until the tomatoes practically dissolve and the sauce is as thick as you want.

Stir in the basil, thyme, oregano, and salt and continue to cook, stirring occasionally, for about 5 minutes, to blend in the flavors of the herbs. Stir in the garlic. Taste and adjust the seasonings if desired.

Variation

To cook this sauce in a pressure cooker, simply sauté the onions in the pressure cooker instead of a soup pot. After you add the tomatoes, fennel, and dried tomatoes, lock on the lid and bring the cooker up to pressure. Adjust the heat to maintain pressure and cook for 1 hour. Let the pressure come down naturally or run cold water over the cooker to speed the process. After the pressure is down, check the sauce, and if it's as thick as you want, stir in the herbs, salt, and garlic. If not yet thick enough, replace the lid, bring the cooker back up to pressure, and cook for 15 to 20 minutes. Check again and, when the tomatoes are completely broken down and the sauce is as thick as you like, stir in the herbs, salt, and garlic. Taste and adjust the seasonings if desired.

Gluten-Free Pastas

Thankfully, a gluten-free diet doesn't have to mean living without pasta. There's an age-old tradition of making pastas from alternative grains, especially in Asia. In fact, some of the most ancient pasta known was a millennia-old millet pasta found in China. That tradition continues to this day, so you should definitely explore and experiment. Here are a few common varieties:

- **Rice noodles.** These come in array of widths and shapes, some broad and flat, and others as thin as vermicelli. The different shapes go by different names, from rice sticks to bifun. They don't have a lot of flavor, so they're great in saucy dishes, where they soak up liquids and become infused with the flavor of the dish.

- **Soba.** For a hearty, earthy flavor, try 100% buckwheat soba. (Read labels carefully, as soba is often made with some wheat.)

- **Bean thread noodles.** Also known as glass or cellophane noodles, these noodles are made from mung bean starch, and as their several names indicate, they're thin and transparent when cooked. Like rice noodles, they're fairly bland, so they're best used in soups and saucy dishes.

Still, you may long for Italian-style pasta from time to time. Fortunately, there are a few great brands of gluten-free pasta available these days, and with all of the current interest in gluten-free eating, it's likely that your choices will soon be multiplied. These days, the best options are made from brown rice or a blend of corn and quinoa, but who knows what the future may bring. Maybe we'll come full circle and millet pasta will reenter the scene. Until then, here are my recommendations regarding Italian-style pastas.

- **Tinkyada** makes great rice pastas; their penne and spirals are especially good.

- **Pastariso** offers terrific lasagna noodles made with rice.

- **Ancient Harvest** makes pasta from a combination of corn and quinoa flour in a wide variety of shapes. For a rainbow of color, try their garden pagodas. Just be forewarned that you need to cook these pastas exactly as directed. Also, any leftovers will harden, so you'll need to reheat them in water (or just mix them with sauce when freshly cooked, and reheat them in their sauce).

- **Alb-Gold** is a German company (see Resources) that makes wonderful pastas from rice or a combination of rice and corn.

- **Eden** offers 100 percent whole buckwheat pasta made with 100 percent buckwheat flour.

Vegan Basil-Walnut Pesto

This pesto is thick, green, and so delicious that I guarantee you won't miss the cheese. Of course it's perfect on pasta, but also try it as a dip, spread, or tossed with hot cooked grains and vegetables.

MAKES ABOUT
1 CUP

———

1 cup walnuts

4 cups tightly packed fresh basil leaves

5 cloves garlic

2 tablespoons extra-virgin olive oil

2 tablespoons umeboshi vinegar

Put the walnuts in a food processor and grind to a coarse meal (see page 24). Add the basil, garlic, oil, and umeboshi vinegar and blend until almost smooth. Taste and adjust the seasonings if desired.

Variation

⚜ Substitute pine nuts for the walnuts, or use a combination of sunflower seeds and walnuts.

Garlicky Hempseed Pesto

Hempseeds and hempseed oil are not only delicious, they're also nutritious, thanks to their generous quantities of healthful omega-3s. You can substitute the more traditional pine nuts and olive oil if you like, but once you taste this version it may become a staple in your summer menu. I like to use Grace cheese in this recipe (and in many others) because it's a locally produced artisanal cheese made with milk from grass-fed cows. Hopefully you can find something similar in your area, but any good Parmesan or Romano would work well here. Toss this thick pesto with warm pasta, or scoop it up with cucumbers and carrots, spread it on tomatoes, or use it as a topping on a zucchini and tomato sauté.

**MAKES ABOUT
2 CUPS**

2 cups grated
Parmesan cheese
(about 8 ounces)

1½ cups tightly
packed fresh basil
leaves

½ cup hempseeds,
rinsed

¼ cup hempseed oil

2 cloves garlic

½ teaspoon sea salt

Combine all of the ingredients in a food processor and blend until almost smooth. Taste and adjust the seasonings if desired.

Cilantro Pesto

Here's a delicious pesto made with cilantro instead of the traditional basil. It's great on any type of noodles, but especially delightful on Asian noodles, such as 100% buckwheat soba or bifun, quick-cooking clear angel hair noodles made from rice flour and potato starch. You may be surprised to learn that it's also a fabulous dip and pizza topping. Spread it on top of a prebaked gluten-free pizza crust and top with sliced bell peppers, olives, and marinated dried tomatoes (see page 171 for a recipe for making your own).

MAKES ABOUT
2 CUPS

½ cup raw almonds, presoaked if you like (see page 78)

½ cup raw sunflower seeds, presoaked if you like (see page 78)

2½ cups tightly packed cilantro leaves

6 cloves garlic

½ cup water

5 tablespoons umeboshi vinegar

Put the almonds in a food processor and grind to a coarse meal (see page 24). Add the sunflower seeds and continue grinding until they too have a texture like coarse meal. Add the cilantro, garlic, water, and umeboshi vinegar and blend until almost smooth. Taste and adjust the seasonings if desired.

Creamy Cilantro Sauce with Ginger

This sprightly sauce is nice on grains, pasta, or grilled vegetables, and especially good atop Coconut Jasmine Rice with Goji Berries and Shiitakes (page 128). I recommend an aged brown rice miso here or, my favorite, Dandelion Leek Miso from South River Miso (see Resources). If you're serving it over pasta, consider 100% buckwheat soba, brown rice spaghetti, or bifun noodles. You could also serve it over rice. It would pair especially well with Madagascar pink rice, basmati, or brown rice.

MAKES ABOUT
2 CUPS

———

2 cups coarsely
chopped cilantro

½ cup cashew
butter (see page 24)

2 tablespoons dark
miso

¼ cup grated fresh
ginger

2 cloves garlic

Combine all of the ingredients in a food processor and blend until completely smooth.

Thai Peanut Sauce

Garlic, mint, and chiles are the essence of Thai cooking, and this versatile sauce is an ideal and easy way to bring their fabulous flavors into your cooking. Experiment with the quantities to suit your tastes or your mood. For more fiery heat, increase the amount of cayenne or chile flakes; to tone it down, add more peanut butter or lime juice. Or you can make it thicker or thinner by varying the amount of water. Try this sauce over tofu, hot or cold noodles, cooked grains, or steamed vegetables, or use it as a salad dressing. Garlic scapes (the flowering tops of garlic) give this sauce a wonderful mild garlic flavor, but if they aren't in season, regular garlic will work just fine.

MAKES ABOUT
2¼ CUPS

---

2 cups cilantro
leaves

¼ cup fresh mint
leaves

3 tablespoons
freshly squeezed
lime juice or rice
vinegar

½ to ⅔ cup peanut
butter (see page 24)

1 cup water

2 garlic scapes, or 2
cloves garlic

1 teaspoon tamari

¼ teaspoon
cayenne or dried
chile flakes

Put all of the ingredients in a food processor in the order listed and blend until smooth and creamy. Taste and adjust the seasonings if desired.

Cranberry-Cherry Sauce

While it's true that gluten isn't an issue with cranberry sauce (at least not any versions I know of), commercial versions are ho-hum, and most of the recipes out there have become all too familiar. Here's an updated version worthy of being served alongside creative, gluten-free dishes like Savory Stuffed Winter Squash (page 72) or Basmati and Wild Rice Pilaf (page 125). Feel free to substitute other dried fruits for some or all of the dried cherries; as always, goji berries would be an especially nutritious choice. Be sure to zest the oranges before you squeeze them; it's much harder to do afterward.

MAKES ABOUT
3 CUPS

———

3 cups fresh or
frozen cranberries

1½ cups dried
pitted cherries

1¼ cups freshly
squeezed orange
juice

3 tablespoons
orange zest

⅓ cup maple syrup

Combine the cranberries, dried cherries, orange juice, and orange zest in a medium-size saucepan over medium-high heat and bring to a boil. Lower the heat and simmer, stirring occasionally, for 5 to 10 minutes, until the cranberries are soft. Stir in the maple syrup. Taste and add more maple syrup if desired. Serve warm.

Moroccan Tahini Sauce or Dressing

One of the benefits of getting familiar with different ingredients and experimenting with them is that you'll develop more confidence in making substitutions based on personal preferences and what's in season. I used to cook for a woman who was allergic to lemons. To her delight (and mine), I found that cumin filled the gap in flavor when I omitted the lemon juice from a typical tahini dressing. Cumin also gives this familiar dressing more of a Middle Eastern flavor. As an added benefit, in Ayurvedic folk medicine cumin seeds are said to be a good remedy for a nervous stomach and digestion.

MAKES ABOUT
3 CUPS
———
3 cloves garlic, or
3 garlic scapes,
coarsely chopped

1 tablespoon plus
1 teaspoon ground
cumin

1½ cups parsley
leaves or cilantro

1 cup tahini

1⅓ cups water

2 teaspoons sea
salt

Put all of the ingredients in a food processor in the order listed and blend until smooth and creamy. Taste and adjust the seasonings if desired.

Avocado Dressing with Garlic Scapes

I love a creamy dressing on salad; don't you? And this one is dairy free! Make this in July, when the garlic scapes are being cut from the garlic plants to help the bulbs grow bigger. If you don't have garlic scapes, substitute regular garlic. Either way, this is delicious not just on salads, but also over grains or pasta.

MAKES ABOUT
1⅓ CUPS
———

⅔ cup water

¼ cup freshly squeezed lemon juice

¼ cup extra-virgin olive oil

½ cup mashed avocado

¾ cup fresh basil leaves

4 garlic scapes, coarsely chopped

¾ teaspoon sea salt

Put all of the ingredients in a blender and blend until smooth and creamy. Taste and adjust the seasonings if desired.

Variations

❧ Swap parsley for the basil.

❧ Substitute regular garlic cloves for the garlic scapes.

Basil-Oregano Vinaigrette

Fresh herbs make this a great dressing for pasta or green salads. For a great summertime main-dish salad, try it on a pasta and bean salad.

MAKES ABOUT
1¼ CUPS

———

½ cup extra-virgin olive oil

½ cup balsamic vinegar

1½ cups fresh basil leaves

½ cup fresh oregano leaves

1 tablespoon sea salt

Put all of the ingredients in a blender and blend until creamy. Taste and adjust the seasonings if desired.

Lemon-Parsley Dressing

This light and refreshing dressing is great on green salads, coleslaw, steamed vegetables, and cooked grains, especially sorghum.

MAKES ABOUT
1¼ CUPS
——————

6 tablespoons extra-virgin olive oil

⅓ cup freshly squeezed lemon juice

1½ cups parsley leaves

2 scallions (white and green parts)

1 tablespoon chopped green bell pepper

1 clove garlic

½ teaspoon sea salt

Put all of the ingredients in a blender or food processor and blend until smooth and creamy. Taste and adjust the seasonings if desired.

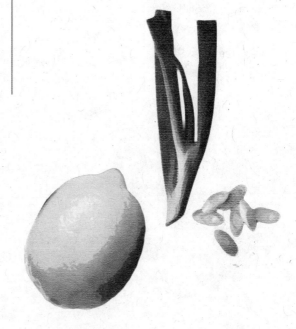

165

Garlicky Basil Dressing

I like the combination of umeboshi vinegar and garlic in this dressing. Umeboshi vinegar isn't technically vinegar (though it can be used like vinegar); it's the tasty liquid left over from the process of pickling umeboshi plums. It has a salty and lemony flavor and can be substituted for those ingredients in many recipes, including hummus. Unlike acidic vinegars, it has an alkalizing effect on digestion. This "vinaigrette" will lend a lively flavor to salads and is also great on cooked sorghum, quinoa, or pasta.

MAKES ABOUT
1 CUP

———

6 tablespoons water

3 tablespoons
extra-virgin olive oil

3 tablespoons
umeboshi vinegar

1 cup tightly packed
fresh basil leaves

8 garlic scapes, or 8
cloves garlic

Put all of the ingredients in a food processor or blender and blend until smooth and creamy. Taste and adjust the seasonings if desired.

Russian Dressing

This Russian dressing doesn't need mayonnaise, sugar, or eggs to be great. Blending tofu with juicy tomatoes, sour pickles, sweet red peppers, and pungent garlic and onion creates a delicious, gorgeous pink dressing that's perfect on a simple salad of lettuce and carrots. It's also tasty on cooked beans and pasta. Avoid the silken tofu that comes in aseptic packages, as the containers contain aluminum and can't be recycled in many communities. If you can't find silken tofu in the refrigerated case, you can use soft regular tofu.

MAKES ABOUT
1¾ CUPS

10 ounces silken tofu

2 tablespoons freshly squeezed lemon juice

2 tablespoons apple cider vinegar

1 cup coarsely chopped tomato

2 tablespoons coarsely chopped dill pickle

2 tablespoons coarsely chopped red bell pepper

2 tablespoons coarsely chopped red onion

1 clove garlic, coarsely chopped

¾ teaspoon sea salt

Put all of the ingredients in a blender or food processor and blend until smooth and creamy. Taste and adjust the seasonings if desired.

Ranch Dressing

Ranch dressing is so popular, but it typically contains a host of unhealthful ingredients. Since many people love it so much, I decided to come up with my own version, substituting tofu for the sour cream and mayonnaise and keeping the other ingredients more or less the same. Use this version in all of the typical ways, and also try spooning some over a baked potato or tossing it in macaroni salad instead of mayonnaise. Although recipes for creamy blended dressings and dips usually call for soft or silken tofu, I like to use firm tofu (and add a bit of water to adjust the texture) because it gives you more nutritional bang for your buck.

MAKES ABOUT 1½ CUPS

---

8 ounces firm tofu, drained

¼ cup water

3 tablespoons honey or maple syrup

2 tablespoons apple cider vinegar

1 tablespoon canola oil

3 tablespoons plus 1 teaspoon coarsely chopped parsley leaves

3 tablespoons coarsely chopped red onion or shallot

1 clove garlic

¼ teaspoon sea salt

Put all of the ingredients in a food processor and blend until smooth and creamy. Taste and adjust the seasonings if desired.

Italian Dressing

This dressing combines balsamic vinegar and red wine vinegar with fresh basil and garlic for an intense flavor that can transform a bowl of rice and beans into a gourmet meal. If you're using it on a green salad, you only need a tablespoon or two per serving, and you may want to tone it down by adding a bit more water.

MAKES ABOUT
1 CUP

———

¼ cup extra-virgin olive oil

¼ cup water

2 tablespoons red wine vinegar

2 tablespoons balsamic vinegar

1 cup fresh basil leaves, tightly packed

6 cloves garlic, pressed or minced very fine

½ teaspoon sea salt

⅛ teaspoon pepper

Put all of the ingredients in a blender or food processor and blend until smooth and creamy. Taste and adjust the seasonings if desired.

169

Basil-Mint Dressing

Fresh basil and mint are a classic summer combination. Here they're blended with fragrant olive oil, lemon juice, and garlic to make an addictive dressing that's equally at home on bean or pasta salads as it is on green salads and other vegetable salads.

MAKES ABOUT
1 CUP

———

½ cup freshly squeezed lemon juice

⅓ cup extra-virgin olive oil

2 cups fresh basil leaves

½ cup fresh mint leaves

5 cloves garlic, or 5 garlic scapes

¼ teaspoon sea salt

Put all of the ingredients in a blender or food processor and blend until smooth and creamy. Taste and adjust the seasonings if desired.

Variations

* Substitute oregano for the mint.
* Try balsamic vinegar in place of the lemon juice.

Marinated Dried Tomatoes

These marinated dried tomatoes are a staple in my kitchen. They're great in dips and roasted vegetable dishes and, of course, as a topping on an endless array of savory dishes, from simple grains to salads to pizzas. You can also use the flavor-infused oil as a condiment, in salad dressings, or for sautéing vegetables or tempeh. If you use all of the tomatoes and have any leftover marinade, you can keep it going by adding more dried tomatoes, garlic, and herbs.

MAKES ABOUT
4 CUPS

———————

1½ cups dried tomatoes

½ cup red or white wine

15 garlic scapes, chopped, or 15 cloves garlic, sliced

1 cup tightly packed basil leaves

About 1⅔ cups extra-virgin olive oil

Place the tomatoes in a bowl or widemouthed quart jar. Pour in the wine and let stand for 2 hours, until the tomatoes absorb most of the wine and soften. Stir gently from time to time to work the tomatoes at the top down into the wine.

Add the garlic and basil, then pour in enough oil to cover everything. Mix and use immediately, or cover with lid and store on your kitchen shelf, where the tomatoes and their flavor-infused oil will keep for at least 1 year.

Variations

❧ Swap balsamic or white wine vinegar for the wine.

❧ Use a different herb or a combination of herbs in place of some or all of the basil: oregano, marjoram, rosemary, and thyme are all good choices.

Fried Dulse

Dulse, a sea vegetable harvested along coasts of the North Atlantic, is rich in iron, calcium, and a wide array of trace minerals. When fried, it has a baconlike flavor and crispness that's easy to love. Use fried dulse as a topping for eggs, grains, soups, stews, and salads.

SERVES 2

2 tablespoons
extra-virgin olive oil

¼ cup dulse

Heat the oil in a medium-size skillet over medium-low heat. Pull the dulse apart, remove any tiny shells, and fry the dulse for about 30 seconds, until it crisps, turns yellow or green, or smells like bacon. Serve immediately.

CHAPTER 8

sweet indulgences

Some folks seem to think that adopting a gluten-free diet means giving up most desserts, especially baked goods. And while you can certainly buy gluten-free cookies and the like, they're no match for homemade when it comes to flavor—and just pure satisfaction. Plus, they can be pretty spendy, and many of them contain questionable ingredients. If you love dessert (and who doesn't?) but think a gluten-free diet means giving up your favorites, this chapter will set you free. And for those avoiding soy and dairy products, no worries: most of the recipes in this chapter don't use them. These are desserts with no apologies. Beyond crisps and fruit pies, you'll find cookies, cakes, a luscious mocha pudding, and a brownie recipe that, in my opinion, outshines all others—gluten free or otherwise. If you're going to indulge, do it in style!

Just like any other time you're in the kitchen, remember to engage your senses while baking. This is how I came up with the recipe for Hazelnut Brownies with Chocolate Chips (page 176). As I pondered what goes with chocolate, I thought of the toasty aroma of hazelnut flour and the richness and tropical flavor of coconut flour. (If you haven't tried baking with coconut flour, you're in for a treat.) And while teff flour has been my favorite for making cookies and piecrusts for over twenty years, I wanted to go a step further and create a dessert that would showcase and build upon its subtle hazelnut and chocolate flavor, so I came up with the recipe for Chocolate Peanut Butter Pie (page 188), where I use hazelnut butter in the teff crust and fill it with a smooth, creamy chocolate pudding enhanced with peanut butter. Over the top? Maybe... Delicious? You bet!

Who needs wheat and its often troublesome gluten when there are so many other great choices. And while it can take some tinkering to create gluten-free cookies and cakes with a good texture, the sky's the limit when it comes to using alternative grains as toppings for fruit crisps where, you can even use nut and seed meals to excellent effect (see the recipes on pages 192 and 193). I could give you a lot more advice and ideas about baking with different grains and flours, but in the end, the most important guide is your own experience, combined with your preferences.

Another fun area to explore is healthy fats. Not that long ago, the primary choices were butter, margarine, shortening, vegetable oil, and (ugh!) lard. These days there are so many interesting oils on the market. Coconut oil is my current favorite, specifically, extra-virgin coconut oil, which imparts a luscious coconut flavor. Although coconut oil has a high percentage of saturated fats, they come in the extremely healthful form of medium-chain triglycerides. We don't need to go into the technical details, but suffice it to say that this allows coconut oil to stand in nicely for traditional hard fats, like shortening and butter. Not that I have a problem with butter! It has a rich and satisfying flavor that's hard to beat. And though nut oils can be expensive, they're very tasty. I especially like hazelnut oil. For a long time, canola was the go-to oil for vegan baking, but I typically don't use it. Not only is it flavorless, if you don't buy organic, it might be genetically modified.

Here are a few tips to make your baking easier, and in some cases, more eco-friendly:

- When you need to measure both a liquid oil and a liquid sweetener, measure the oil first (including melted coconut oil and butter). Then, when you measure sticky liquid sweeteners like honey or maple syrup, they'll slide out of the measuring cup quickly and cleanly. For the same reason, when making a recipe that calls for both oil and nut butter, it's best to measure the oil first.

- When a recipe calls for melted coconut oil, I find the easiest way to melt it is in a small skillet. Then, if you need to oil a baking sheet or other pan, you can just clean out the skillet with a pastry brush and use the brush to oil the pan.

- You'll read many recipes that call for mixing wet and dry ingredients separately, then combining them. In my experience, this isn't necessary, and it just dirties another dish. Most of the time, you can just mix everything together in one bowl.

- In the recipes in this chapter, I've organized ingredients lists so that the information is presented in a uniform way to make things easier for you. But when I'm cooking, I usually add the ingredients in whatever order I like. You should feel free to do the same. One caveat: If you're making a batter that uses egg, whisk the egg first, then add the remaining ingredients.

Hazelnut Brownies
with Chocolate Chips

This is the best brownie recipe I know of—gluten free or otherwise. Enjoy them warm out of the oven. Or, in the unlikely event that you have leftovers, rest assured that they get better every day.

SERVES 6 TO 8

2 eggs

1 cup apple or pear juice

¼ cup melted extra-virgin coconut oil or butter

½ cup maple syrup

1 teaspoon vanilla extract

¾ cup finely ground raw hazelnuts (skins on) or hazelnut flour (see page 24)

½ cup cocoa powder

⅓ cup brown rice flour

¼ cup coconut flour

1 teaspoon baking powder

½ teaspoon sea salt

¾ cup dark chocolate chips

Preheat the oven to 350°F. Lightly oil a 9-inch round pan or a standard loaf pan.

Whisk the eggs in a large bowl. Add all of the remaining ingredients, holding back ¼ cup of chocolate chips, and stir until thoroughly combined. Pour the batter into the prepared pan, scraping the bowl to get every last speck of chocolaty goodness. Decorate the top with the remaining chocolate chips.

Bake for about 30 minutes, until a toothpick inserted in the center comes out clean (or with only melted chocolate on it). Cool for at least 30 minutes before slicing and eating—if you can wait that long!

Cashew Butter Chocolate Chip Cookies

I encourage you to think of the recipes in this chapter (and through-out the book) as master recipes, providing a structure that you can use to create your own variations. That's exactly what my neighbor Mara did to create these delicious cookies. Starting with the recipe for Peanut Butter–Chocolate Chip Cookies in my cookbook *Going Wild in the Kitchen*, she swapped cashew butter for the peanut butter, replaced ½ cup of the teff flour with coconut flour, and added an egg. The possibilities are endless, which is always a good thing, especially when it comes to gluten-free cookies.

MAKES ABOUT 2
DOZEN COOKIES

1 cup teff flour

½ cup coconut flour

½ teaspoon sea salt

1 cup cashew butter
(see page 24)

½ cup butter or
extra-virgin coconut
oil, softened or
at warm room
temperature

½ cup maple syrup

1 egg

½ cup dark
chocolate chips

Preheat the oven to 350°F.

Put the teff flour, coconut flour, and salt in a large bowl.

Put the cashew butter, butter, maple syrup, and egg in a food processor and blend until creamy. Add the mixture to the flour, along with the chocolate chips, and stir until well combined.

Shape the dough into walnut-size balls and place them on an unoiled baking sheet about ½ inch apart. Gently flatten the cookies with the tines of a fork.

Bake 10 to 15 minutes, or until the cookies lose their shine. Let the cookies cool on the baking sheet for at least 10 minutes before handling. They will be soft when they come out of the oven but will crisp up when they cool.

Variation

⚜ Swap carob chips for the chocolate chips.

177

Hazelnut Butter Cookies

These are one of my favorite cookies. They're rich, satisfying, and, if you make them with coconut oil, vegan—and proof that sometimes the simplest things are also the best.

MAKES ABOUT 3
DOZEN COOKIES

2 cups teff flour

½ teaspoon sea salt

1 cup hazelnut butter (see page 24)

½ cup extra-virgin coconut oil or butter, softened or at warm room temperature

½ cup maple syrup

Preheat the oven to 350°F.

Put the flour and salt in a large bowl.

Put the hazelnut butter, oil, and maple syrup in a food processor and blend until creamy. Add the mixture to the flour and stir until well combined.

Shape the dough into walnut-size balls and place them on an unoiled baking sheet about ½ inch apart. Gently flatten the cookies with the tines of a fork.

Bake for 10 to 15 minutes, until the cookies lose their shine. Let the cookies cool on the baking sheet for at least 10 minutes before handling. They will be soft when they come out of the oven but will crisp up when they cool.

Maple Sugar Cookies

These taste just like my Grandma Ethel's sugar cookies, but they're made with rice flour and maple sugar.

MAKES ABOUT
18 COOKIES

1½ cups brown rice
flour

¼ teaspoon sea salt

5 tablespoons extra-
virgin coconut oil,
softened or at warm
room temperature

½ cup maple sugar

1 egg

½ teaspoon almond
extract

Preheat the oven to 350°F. Oil a baking sheet.

Put the flour and salt in a bowl.

Put the oil and maple sugar in a food processor and blend until creamy. Add the egg and almond extract and blend until well mixed. Add the mixture to the flour and stir until well combined.

Shape the dough into walnut-size balls and place them about ½ inch apart on the prepared baking sheet. Gently flatten the cookies with the tines of a fork.

Bake for about 10 minutes, until light brown. Cool for at least 10 minutes before eating.

Date and Coconut Cookies

Sweet and scented with vanilla, these are also high in iron, making them the ultimate woman's cookie!

MAKES ABOUT 3 DOZEN COOKIES

2 cups teff flour

⅔ cup ground flaxseeds

⅔ cup shredded unsweetened coconut

1 teaspoon ground cinnamon

½ teaspoon sea salt

⅓ cup melted extra-virgin coconut oil

⅔ cup maple syrup

⅔ cup chopped pitted dates

⅓ cup raisins

1 tablespoon vanilla extract

Preheat the oven to 350°F. Lightly oil a baking sheet.

Put all of the ingredients in a mixing bowl and stir until well combined.

Shape the dough into walnut-size balls and place them on the prepared baking sheet about ½ inch apart. Gently flatten the cookies with the tines of a fork.

Bake for about 10 minutes, until the cookies lose their shine. Let the cookies cool on the baking sheet for at least 10 minutes before handling. They will be soft when they come out of the oven but will crisp up when they cool.

Honey Hazelnut Treats

Easy to make and fun to eat, these sensational raw food treats are also excellent party fare. In addition to being gluten free, they have minimal added sweetening and aren't even baked, which is especially nice in hot weather, when you may not want to turn on the oven. Cacao powder is simply cocoa powder that wasn't subjected to high heat during processing, so it qualifies as a raw food. Cacao nibs are simply roasted, cracked cacao beans.

MAKES ABOUT 2 DOZEN TREATS

1 cup raw hazelnuts (skins on)

1 cup pitted dates

¼ cup unsweetened shredded coconut

¼ cup honey

1 tablespoon vanilla extract

Pinch of sea salt

2 tablespoons cacao nibs

1 tablespoon raw cacao powder

Put the hazelnuts in a food processor and grind to a coarse meal (see page 24). Add the dates, coconut, honey, vanilla, and salt and blend until well mixed.

Sprinkle the cacao nibs and cacao powder onto a large plate. Shape the hazelnut mixture into walnut-size balls, and roll the balls around on the plate until evenly coated. Arrange the balls on a platter and serve immediately, or store them in an airtight container in the refrigerator.

Lemon Poppy Seed Cake

This recipe is a good example of how to use your creativity and preferences to create new variations. When I was dreaming up how to do a
gluten-free take on the classic combination of lemon and poppy seeds,
I thought almonds and coconut would be a delicious complement. The
result is a cake that's moist and scrumptious, with a fun interplay of
flavors and textures. Zest the lemon before you squeeze the juice; it
works so much better that way.

SERVES 6 TO 8

2 eggs

1 cup apple or peach juice

¼ cup melted extra-virgin coconut oil

½ cup maple syrup

1 tablespoon lemon zest

¼ cup freshly squeezed lemon juice

1 tablespoon vanilla extract

¾ cup finely ground raw almonds or almond flour (see page 24)

½ cup brown rice flour

⅓ cup poppy seeds

⅓ cup coconut flour

1 teaspoon baking powder

½ teaspoon sea salt

Preheat the oven to 350°F. Generously oil a standard loaf pan or 9-inch round cake pan.

Whisk the eggs in a large bowl. Add the remaining ingredients and stir until thoroughly combined.

Pour the batter into the prepared pan and bake for 40 to 50 minutes, until a toothpick inserted in the center comes out clean. Let the cake cool for at least 30 minutes before slicing and serving.

Millet Apple Raisin Cake

Millet is a naturally sweet grain, and after cooking, it sets up and is sliceable. My daughter Emily loved this cake as a child—still does twenty years later. Not only is it quick and easy to make, it's extremely healthful. In fact, you need not enjoy it just for dessert; instead of pouring it into a pan to set up, you can eat it hot, as a porridge. And as you can see from the variations below, it's also a very versatile dish. Experiment and tweak it to your liking!

SERVES ABOUT 6

1 cup millet, rinsed

3 cups apple juice

1 cup raisins

Pinch of sea salt

Combine the millet, juice, raisins, and salt in a medium-size saucepan over high heat. Bring to a boil, then lower heat, cover, and simmer for about 20 minutes, until all of the juice is absorbed and the millet is tender. Give it a stir, and then taste it; if the millet is still crunchy, add more juice, cover, and simmer for about 3 minutes, then check the tenderness again.

Pour the mixture into a standard loaf pan and let it cool for about 1 hour, until set. Slice and serve. Store any leftovers in the refrigerator.

Variations

- Use a combination of other fresh or dried fruits, such as pears, apples, or apricots. Small fruits are fine as is, but you may want to chop fruits that come in larger pieces.

- Try different fruit juices.

- Stir in about 1 teaspoon of ground cinnamon or vanilla extract before pouring the batter into the loaf pan.

- Use corn grits in place of some or all of the millet.

- To use a pressure cooker, just put all of the ingredients in the pressure cooker and lock the lid. Bring up to pressure over high heat, then adjust the heat to maintain pressure and cook for 15 minutes.

Chocolate Mousse Pie in a Hazelnut Crust

Chocolate and hazelnuts are a classic combination and one of my favorites. Here, the sweet hazelnuts form the perfect backdrop for a silky mousse that tastes much richer and more decadent than it really is. That said, feel free to have delicious fun pairing this filling with other piecrust recipes in this chapter. Although silken tofu so often comes in aseptic packages, it's best to avoid these, as the packaging contains aluminum and, in many communities, isn't recyclable. Look for silken tofu in the refrigerator case, and if you can't find it, use soft regular tofu instead (in which case you may want to add more water or sweetener to the filling). Cacao powder is simply cocoa powder that wasn't subjected to high heat during processing, so it qualifies as a raw food. Cacao powder has more vitamins and antioxidants than cocoa, because cocoa is heated, which gives it that familiar hot cocoa aroma. Both are very delicious, and you can substitute one for the other.

Variations

- Substitute butter, light olive oil, light sesame oil, or canola oil for the hazelnut oil.
- Swap carob powder for the cocoa.
- For a delicious raw pie crust, forgo baking it and just add the filling after you press it into the pan.

SERVES 6 TO 8

Crust

1½ cups raw
hazelnuts (skins on)

2 tablespoons
hazelnut oil or
melted extra-virgin
coconut oil

¼ cup maple syrup

¼ teaspoon sea salt

Filling

16 ounces silken
tofu

¼ cup cocoa
powder or raw
cacao powder

⅓ cup maple sugar

1 tablespoons
vanilla extract

2 tablespoons
unsweetened
shredded coconut

Preheat oven to 375°F. Lightly oil a
9-inch pie pan.

To make the crust, put the hazelnuts
in a food processor and grind into a
flour (see page 24). Add the hazelnut
oil, maple syrup, and salt, and pulse to
form a soft dough.

Transfer the dough to the prepared pie
pan and use your fingers to press it out
in an even layer over the bottom and
sides of the pan. Poke a few holes in
the dough with a fork. Bake for about
10 minutes, until lightly browned. Let
the crust cool and set up for about 15
minutes, until cool enough to touch.

Meanwhile, make the filling. Put the
tofu, cocoa powder, maple sugar, and
vanilla in the food processor (no need
to clean it, really) and blend until
smooth and creamy. Taste and add
more cocoa or maple sugar if desired.

Pour the filling into the crust, smooth
the top, and sprinkle with the coconut.
Serve immediately or, if you prefer it
cold, refrigerate the pie for at least 2
hours before serving. Store any leftovers
in the refrigerator.

Chocolate Peanut Butter Pie

Peanut butter and hazelnut butter are both great partners for chocolate, so why not team all of them up? The result is a pie so rich and satisfying that it's hard to believe it's this easy to make. This crust is quite
different from the one used for Chocolate Mousse Pie in a Hazelnut
Crust (page 186), but the two are similar in one important regard: Both
are vegan, and so much less fussy than a traditional pie crust. As
explained in the recipe for Chocolate Mousse Pie in a Hazelnut Crust,
you can substitute soft regular tofu for the silken tofu, but if you do so,
you may want to add a bit more sweetener to the filling.

⊷ **Chocolate Peanut Pudding:** Although the teff crust couldn't
be easier to make, if you're strapped for time, or if you simply
prefer pudding, skip making the crust and serve the filling as is,
hopefully in pudding cups.

SERVES 6 TO 8

Crust

2 cups teff flour

½ cup maple syrup

2 tablespoons hazelnut butter (see page 24)

5 teaspoons melted extra-virgin coconut oil

¼ teaspoon sea salt

Filling

1½ cups dark chocolate chips

1 pound silken tofu

3 tablespoons peanut butter (see page 24)

2 teaspoons vanilla extract

Chocolate chips for decorating (optional)

Preheat oven to 375° F degrees. Lightly oil a 9-inch pie pan.

To make the crust, put the teff flour, maple syrup, hazelnut butter, oil, and salt in a medium-size bowl and stir until well combined.

Transfer the dough to the prepared pie pan and use your fingers to press it out in an even layer over the bottom and sides of the pan. Poke a few holes in the dough with a fork. Bake for about 10 minutes, until it loses its shine. Let the crust cool while you make the filling. (Leave the oven on.)

To make the filling, start by melting the chocolate. You can use a double boiler if you like, but I find that it works just fine to melt it in a heavy 9-inch frying pan over low heat, stirring occasionally, for about 5 minutes.

Transfer the melted chocolate to a food processor. Add the tofu, peanut butter, and vanilla and blend until smooth and creamy. Taste and add more melted chocolate if desired.

Pour the filling into the crust and smooth the top, then decorate the top with chocolate chips if you like. Bake for about 5 minutes, until the edges of the filling darken slightly. You can serve the pie as soon as it's cool enough to handle or let it cool to room temperature. Or if you prefer it cold, refrigerate the pie for at least 2 hours before serving. Store any leftovers in the refrigerator.

Granny Smith Apple Crumb Pie

This delicious pie is perfect for winter holiday fare. And because it's so easy to make, it's a nice way to lighten your load when you'll be doing a lot of other cooking. In the unlikely event that you have any leftovers, it's also great for breakfast, served topped with a dollop of yogurt. Dates balance the tartness of Granny Smith apples beautifully, but you can make endless variations on this pie by choosing almost any fruit that's in season and pairing it with whatever dried fruit seems appealing.

SERVES 6 TO 8

Crust

2 cups teff flour

½ cup melted extra-virgin coconut oil or butter

½ cup maple syrup

½ teaspoon sea salt

Filling

¼ cup water

3 Granny Smith apples, thinly sliced

¾ cup pitted dates

1½ teaspoons ground cinnamon

Pinch of sea salt

Preheat the oven to 375°F. Lightly oil a 9-inch pie pan.

To make the crust, combine the teff flour, oil, maple syrup, and salt in a medium-size bowl and stir until well combined. Reserve ½ cup of the mixture to use as a crumb topping.

Transfer the dough to the prepared pie pan and use your fingers to press it out in an even layer over the bottom and sides of the pan. Poke a few holes in the dough with a fork. Bake for about 10 minutes, until it loses its shine.

Meanwhile, make the filling. Put the water, apples, dates, cinnamon, and salt in a medium-size saucepan over medium-low heat and simmer, stirring occasionally, for about 5 minutes, until the apples soften. Taste and add more cinnamon or adjust the sweetness if desired.

Pour the filling into the crust and crumble the reserved dough over the top. Bake for about 10 minutes, until the crumbs turn a slightly darker brown. Let the pie cool for at least 30 minutes before serving.

Leslie's Gluten-Free Peach Pie

Remarkably delicious, this pie is fun and easy to make. For a light-colored piecrust like the luscious pie on the cover of this cookbook, use ivory teff flour; for a chocolate-brown piecrust use brown teff flour. Both are equally scrumptious. Serve the pie warm, or top it with ice cream, a non-dairy frozen dessert, or whipped cream. You could even serve it with a dollop of yogurt for breakfast.

SERVES 6 TO 8

Crust

2 cups teff flour

½ cup melted extra-virgin coconut oil or butter

½ cup maple syrup

1 tablespoon vanilla extract

½ teaspoon sea salt

Filling

5 ripe peaches, thinly sliced

1 tablespoon maple sugar or date sugar

1½ teaspoons cinnamon

Preheat the oven to 375°F. Lightly oil a 9-inch pie pan.

To make the crust, combine the teff flour, oil, maple syrup, vanilla, and salt in a medium-size bowl and stir until well combined. Reserve ½ cup of the mixture to use as a crumb topping.

Transfer the dough to the prepared pie pan and use your fingers to press it out in an even layer over the bottom and sides of the pan. Poke a few holes in the dough with a fork. Bake for about 10 minutes, until it loses it shine.

Put the peaches in the baked piecrust. Sprinkle the maple sugar and cinnamon over the peaches.

Crumble the reserved dough over the peaches. Bake for about 10 minutes, until the crumbs turn a slightly darker brown, and the peaches are tender to your liking.

Let the pie cool for at least 30 minutes before serving.

Variations

❧ Simmer the peaches, sugar, and cinnamon, along with a bit of water, before putting them in the piecrust.

❧ Make a topless peach pie by using the crust recipe on page 192.

Topless Blueberry Pie

This beautiful vegan pie is quick and easy to make, and even easier to love. Feel free to swap other seasonal fruits for blueberries, such as cherries or peaches. Date sugar, made from crushed dried dates, has a coarse texture, which works just fine in this recipe, but if you'd like it finer, just grind it in a food processor or coffee grinder.

SERVES 6 TO 8

Crust

1½ cups teff flour

½ cup date sugar

½ cup canola oil or melted extra-virgin coconut oil

⅓ cup water

½ teaspoon sea salt

Filling

2 cups fresh or frozen blueberries

Pinch of sea salt

¼ cup brown rice syrup

1 tablespoon arrowroot or kudzu powder

¼ cup cold water

Preheat the oven to 375°F. Lightly oil a 9-inch pie pan.

To make the crust, put the teff flour, date sugar, oil, water, and salt in a medium-size bowl and stir until well combined.

Transfer the dough to the prepared pie pan and use your fingers to press it out in an even layer over the bottom and sides of the pan. Poke a few holes in the dough with a fork. Bake for about 10 minutes, until lightly browned.

Meanwhile, make the filling. Combine the blueberries and salt in a medium-size saucepan over medium-low heat and simmer for 3 minutes. If you feel you must stir, do so gently to keep the blueberries whole. Gently stir in the syrup and simmer for just a moment longer. (Keeping the cooking time short will also help keep the blueberries whole.)

Dissolve the arrowroot powder in the cold water, then stir the slurry into the berries. Cook for about 1 minute, until slightly thickened. Taste and, if you'd like a sweeter flavor, add more syrup.

Pour the filling into the crust. Let the pie cool for at least 20 minutes, until the filling sets up, before serving.

Apple Coconut Crisp

Take your pick of several flours to make this delicious apple crisp. I like to use Gala, Cortland, or McIntosh apples because they are my local favorites and bake quickly; if apples grow in your area, I encourage you to experiment with local varieties and find which you like best. Enjoy this crisp for dessert, and if any is left over, top it with maple yogurt for a great breakfast.

SERVES 6 TO 8

4 cups sliced apples

2 cups rolled oats

½ cup ground flaxseeds

⅓ cup melted extra-virgin coconut oil or butter

⅓ cup maple syrup or brown rice syrup

1 teaspoon ground cinnamon

½ teaspoon sea salt

1 cup apple juice

Preheat the oven to 350°F.

Spread the apples over the bottom of an 8-inch square baking dish. Put the rolled oats, flaxseeds, oil, maple syrup, cinnamon, and salt in a medium-size bowl and stir until thoroughly combined. (You may want to use your hands.) Crumble the mixture over the apples, then pour the juice over the top.

Bake for about 30 minutes, until the topping is crisp and the apples are tender. Serve warm.

Variations

◄ Use any combination of fresh, dried, or frozen fruits. Whatever fruit you use, you'll need to bake for at least 30 minutes so the topping crisps up.

◄ Try other flavors of fruit juice.

◄ Substitute teff flour, brown rice flour, or sorghum flour for the ground flaxseeds; or try ground almonds or ground hazelnuts (see page 24 for more information on grinding nuts).

Pear and Cranberry Crisp

Lovely and versatile, this fruit crisp offers you plenty of options. You can make it with different flours or swap other seasonal fruits every time you make it. Enjoy this crisp for dessert, topped with whipped cream or ice cream, and if any is left over, top it with maple yogurt for a great breakfast.

SERVES 6 TO 8

3 Bartlett pears, cored and sliced

¾ cup fresh or frozen cranberries

2 cups rolled oats

½ cup teff flour

⅓ cup melted extra-virgin coconut oil

⅓ cup maple syrup

1 tablespoon vanilla extract

1 teaspoon ground cinnamon

½ teaspoon sea salt

1 cup apple juice

Preheat the oven to 375°F.

Spread the pears and cranberries over the bottom of a 9 by 13-inch baking dish. Put the rolled oats, flour, oil, maple syrup, vanilla, cinnamon, and salt in a medium-size bowl and stir until thoroughly combined. (You may want to use your hands.) Crumble the mixture over the fruit, then pour the juice over the top.

Bake for about 30 minutes, until the topping is crisp and the fruit is tender. Serve warm.

Variations

⁕ Substitute other seasonal fruits: peaches, blueberries, strawberries, or apples would all be great choices. The baking time may vary from 20 to 30 minutes; it's done when the topping is crisp and the fruit is tender.

⁕ Try other flavors of fruit juice.

⁕ Substitute brown rice flour or sorghum flour for the teff flour, or try ground almonds, ground hazelnuts, or ground flaxseeds (see page 24 for more information on grinding nuts and seeds).

Mocha Coconut Rice Pudding

This isn't your everyday mocha; coconut milk and cinnamon sticks give this rice pudding an exotic and especially enticing flavor, and the Madagascar pink rice adds an exotic tropical flavor, but you could use long-grain brown rice or brown basmati rice, if you like; just be sure to increase the cooking time to 40 minutes. For a beautiful decorative touch, garnish each serving with fresh seasonal berries.

SERVES 4 TO 6

¾ cup Madagascar pink rice

1 (14-ounce) can coconut milk

2 cups water

2 cinnamon sticks

Pinch of sea salt

3 tablespoons cocoa powder

2 tablespoons finely ground dark roast coffee

3 tablespoons maple syrup

1 tablespoon vanilla extract

1 cup raspberries or sliced strawberries, for garnish (optional)

Put the rice and coconut milk in a medium-size saucepan. Pour some of the water into the coconut milk can and swish it around, then pour it into the pan; if needed, repeat with more of the water so you get every last drop of the coconut milk's goodness into the pan. Once all of the water is added to the pan, add the cinnamon sticks and salt and stir to combine.

Bring to a boil over high heat, then lower the heat, stir in the cocoa powder and coffee, and simmer for about 20 minutes, until all of the liquid is absorbed. Stir in the maple syrup and vanilla extract. Serve immediately, garnished with the berries if you like. Store any leftovers in the refrigerator.

Sesame Almond Bars

This crunchy and sweet confection is the perfect alternative to sugary peanut brittle. Enjoy these bars for snacking and with tea. Using kelp instead of salt adds minerals and enhances the flavor of the other ingredients. For this recipe, I recommend kelp flakes from BC Kelp (see Resources), harvested off the shore of British Columbia. Special thanks to Kacie Loparto of She Sells Seaweed for sharing a version of this recipe in my Cooking with Sea Vegetables class, and for being so open to my new variation.

MAKES ABOUT 16 BARS

¼ cup olive oil

½ cup brown rice syrup

1 cup sesame seeds

½ cup chopped raw almonds

¼ cup kelp flakes

Preheat the oven to 350°F. Line a baking sheet with parchment paper.

Put the oil and syrup in a medium-size saucepan over medium-high heat and bring to a boil. Lower the heat and simmer for about 5 minutes, until the mixture begins to foam. Turn off the heat add the sesame seeds, almonds, and kelp, and stir until thoroughly combined.

Transfer the mixture to the prepared pan and lay another sheet of parchment paper on top. Use a rolling pin to gently spread and flatten the mixture.

Bake for about 10 minutes, until crisp. Peel off the parchment paper and break the crunch into rectangular pieces. Serve immediately, or store in an airtight container at room temperature.

glossary of ingredients

This glossary offers information on some of the more unusual ingredients in the recipes. For information on grains and flours, see chapter 1, Meet the Gluten-Free Grains.

Arrowroot powder, derived from the root of a plant native to the West Indies, can be added to flour to make baked goods lighter and fluffier. It can also be used as a thickener for stews, sauces, and puddings.

Brown rice syrup is thick and amber colored. Made from cooked brown rice, it is about half as sweet as sugar. Use it in sauces, salad dressings, puddings, frostings, and pie fillings, and as a topping for pancakes.

Coconut oil is a cholesterol-free saturated fat with numerous health benefits. This semisolid white oil, extracted from fresh coconuts, enlivens both savory and sweet dishes. Use it like olive oil or butter in cooking and baking. I prefer extra-virgin coconut oil because I love the taste of coconut. If you don't want the coconut flavor, use a refined coconut oil. As always with oils, be sure to use organic. Because oils are concentrated (a little oil being made from a lot of source ingredients), toxins in the source ingredient may be more concentrated in the oil.

Dulse is a soft, leafy, reddish purple-brown sea vegetable harvested along coasts of the North Atlantic. It melts in your mouth and makes a wonderful snack, and kids love it. Fried, it tastes almost like bacon and is delicious served on the side with eggs or as a crisp garnish. You can also add it to oatmeal, soups, stews, or bean dishes; or rinse it and add it to a salad in place of spinach. Like most sea vegetables, dulse is a good source of vitamins and minerals; a single serving (just 7 grams) contains 42 percent of the daily value for vitamin B_6, 23 percent of the daily value for vitamin B_{12}, and 19 percent of the daily value for iron.

Garlic scapes, the green stem and flowering tops of garlic, are cut off by growers to encourage the garlic bulb to grow larger. Lucky for us, they are harvested in summer, giving us fresh garlic to use while we wait for the bulbs to mature in autumn. No need to peel them, either; just chop them up like scallions and add them to dips, dressings, pesto, stir-fries, or anywhere you'd use garlic. They're a nice crunchy vegetable with mild garlic flavor and tasty in their own right. However, their season is fairly short, and unless you grow your own or shop at a farmer's market or a well-stocked natural food store, they can be difficult to find. No problem! Just substitute 1 clove of garlic for each garlic scape.

Ghee, like clarified butter, is made by simmering butter and then pouring off the butterfat. This removes the milk solids and makes the butter easier to digest. Ghee doesn't require refrigeration and can be used like butter for high-heat cooking, as in frying, roasting, and grilling. Although you can purchase ghee, why not make it yourself? It's so easy. For the method, see page 86.

Goji berries, also known as wolfberries, are small, red berries revered in Chinese medicine for promoting health, vitality, stamina, and longevity. Typically sold dried, they're loaded with vitamins and minerals, especially vitamin C, iron, and beta-carotene. Use them like raisins in porridges, pilafs, and baked goods. If you don't have goji berries on hand, you can substitute other small dried fruits, such as raisins or dried cranberries

Hempseeds have a softer texture than sesame seeds and a mild flavor. They are a complete protein and also rich in fiber, vitamins, minerals, and omega-3, omega-6, and omega-9 fatty acids. Try them sprinkled on grains, granola, salads, yogurt, soups, and dips, or mix them in with flour when baking.

Kelp is a thin, leafy variety of kombu sea vegetable harvested off the coast in the northern Atlantic and northern Pacific. When toasted and ground, it makes a great condiment that's especially good on popcorn and soups. Contact BC Kelp (see Resources) to purchase a wonderful variety that has a crisp texture like a potato chip and doesn't need to be toasted before grinding for use as a condiment. The Atlantic variety is great for making beans from scratch, or for longer cooking techniques where it enhances flavors as it melts into soups and stews.

Kudzu, made from the root of a plant native to Japan and China, is used as a thickener for soups, stews, sauces, jellies, and jam. In Oriental medicine, it's recommended for its calming antacid effect on digestion. It usually comes in small chunks that you need to dissolve in cold water before adding to recipes.

Maca root comes from the Andes of Bolivia and Peru, where it has been used for thousands of years to boost stamina. It's loaded with vitamins, minerals, amino acids, and healthy fats and is thought to boost libido and immune system function and help combat stress. Typically available dried as a powder or flour, it has a pleasing earthy, nutty flavor. The flavor is strong, so little goes a long way; for a hint of its sophisticated flavor, you can add a tablespoon to everything from baked goods to smoothies to stews. But if you don't have any on hand, don't let that stop you from making any of the pastry recipes in this book that call for it. Just substitute an equal amount of flour for the maca.

Miso is a salty and sometimes sweet fermented paste made from beans, grains, or a combination of the two, along with sea salt. Some varieties also include sea vegetables, spices, and even dandelion greens. Light, mellow sweet and white varieties, aged from 3 to 6 months, have a subtle flavor that's excellent for salad dressings, creamy sauces, dips, and delicate soups. Darker varieties, aged for 1 to 3 years, such as hearty brown rice miso, red miso, and hatcho miso, are saltier, stronger in flavor, and delicious in soups, casseroles, and stews.

Nori is a delicate purplish-black sea vegetable most familiar in the form of sheets used for sushi rolls. When toasted and crumbled, nori is a tasty garnish and condiment. Of all of the seaweeds, it is the highest in protein and vitamins A and C and is a good source of all the B vitamins. It also has a relatively low sodium content.

Sea salt contains more trace minerals and less sodium chloride than commercial salt, which has added iodine, as well as chemicals used to stabilize the salt or keep it flowing freely. Salt is undergoing a renaissance these days and a lot of interesting varieties are available, from Celtic Sea Salt to Himalayan varieties to solar-dried versions. Experiment with different salts for different purposes to discover which you like best.

Sesame oil is, obviously, made from sesame seeds. Just be aware that there are two basic types: Toasted sesame oil is highly flavorful and typically isn't used for cooking; rather, it's used in dressings and for drizzling on soups and stir-fries to give them an Asian accent. Plain sesame oil has a lighter aroma and flavor and tolerates moderately high heat, making it a good choice for sautéing, baking, and braising. It's also great in dressings and dips. I always use unrefined, organic sesame oil, which has a superior nutritional profile and a richer flavor and color than refined varieties. And because oils are concentrated (a little oil being made from a lot of source ingredients), toxins in the source ingredient may be more concentrated in the oil.

Tahini, a paste made by grinding sesame seeds, is a great source of iron and calcium and a common ingredient in Middle Eastern cooking. Add tahini to sauces, spreads, and stews for a rich, creamy texture and flavor.

Tamari is a natural soy sauce made without wheat. When made traditionally, it's the liquid that rises to the surface during miso making; however, these days it's more often manufactured directly—to save time, and because more tamari is sold than could be generated via miso production. Use it anywhere you'd like a salty flavor: on grains, as a seasoning in stir-fries, stews, and soups, and so on.

Tempeh is made from cooked and fermented soybeans, sometimes with other ingredients, including grains, so read the label carefully to be sure it's gluten free. It has a firm, tender, meaty texture. It's high in protein, easy to digest, cholesterol free, delicious, and extremely versatile. You can sauté, bake, broil, steam, or simmer it, and it combines well with a wide variety of vegetables, herbs, and spices. It's a great addition to soups, stews, casseroles, sushi, and sandwiches.

Tofu is a fairly familiar ingredient these days, but there are a few points to keep in mind. First, avoid purchasing tofu in aseptic packaging; the packages contain aluminum and also can't be recycled in many communities. Tofu comes in many textures. Extra firm is my favorite for stir-fries and sautés. Firm contains a little more water. Soft and silken tofu are great for puddings, pie fillings, and creamy dressings.

Umeboshi paste is a puree of umeboshi plums: small pickled plums that are aged for several years. They have a distinctive flavor that combines sweet, sour, and salty. Umeboshi paste is often spread on toasted nori or sushi rice when making nori rolls. You can also use it instead of lemon juice and sea salt to season salad dressings, sauces, and dips.

Umeboshi vinegar, also known as ume vinegar, can be used in place of tamari or lemon and salt. It has a sour (lemony) and salty flavor and a deep ruby color. Although it isn't actually vinegar, it can be used in the same way. It is the juices extracted during the process of making pickled umeboshi plums, together with shiso (beefsteak) leaves and sea salt. For a quick, delicious salad dressing, try olive oil and umeboshi vinegar, or sesame oil, umeboshi vinegar, and rice vinegar.

resources

---

ingredients

Alb-Gold North America Inc
Attn: Egon Flad, General Manager
P.O. Box 1353
444 E. 82nd Street #14C
New York, NY 10028
212-861-7212
www.alb-gold.com

This German company, which is dedicated to organic agriculture, makes and distributes a full line of pastas, including gourmet pastas made from rice or a combination of rice and corn.

BC KELP
P.O. Box 274
Prince Rupert, British Columbia
V8J 3P3, Canada
250-622-7085
www.bckelp.com

BC Kelp offers a delicious variety of kelp in flakes, powder, and whole form, as well as wakame, kombu, seaweed fertilizer, and sea vegetable bath products.

Bob's Red Mill Whole Grain Store
5000 SE International Way
Milwaukie, OR 97222
800-349-2173
www.bobsredmill.com

Bob's Red Mill offers a wide variety of gluten-free products: whole grains, flakes, flours, and more—including nut flours. Their website also offers recipes and links to forums and FAQs on gluten-free cooking. Most natural food stores and many well-stocked supermarkets carry a wide variety of products from Bob's Red Mill, but if you can't find what you're looking for, you can order from the website.

Frontier Natural Products Co-op
P.O. Box 299
Norway, IA 52318
800-669-3275
www.frontiercoop.com

Frontier offers a full line of fair trade, certified organic dried herbs, spices, vanilla, flaxseeds, sea vegetables, and more.

glutenfree.com
P.O. Box 840
Glastonbury, CT 06033
800-291-8386
www.glutenfree.com

This is a good source for gluten-free grains, flours, pastas, condiments, baked goods and other prepared foods, and more, including recipes, resources, and information.

Gluten-Free Mall, Inc.

4927 Sonoma Highway, Suite C1
Santa Rosa, CA 95409
866-575-3720
www.glutenfreemall.com

This is another good source for gluten-free grains, flours, pastas, condiments, baked goods and other prepared foods, and more, including recipes, resources, and information.

Gold Mine Natural Food Company

7805 Arjons Drive
San Diego, CA 92126
800-475-3663
www.goldminenaturalfood.com

In addition to offering grains, flours, beans, sweeteners, sea vegetables, miso, umeboshi products, and kudzu, Gold Mine is also one of the few sources for Ohsawa pots, a type of ceramic crock used to cook grains in a pressure cooker (see page 35).

Living Tree Community Foods

P.O. Box 10082
Berkeley, CA 94709
800-260-5534
www.livingtreecommunity.com

Living Tree offers a full line of nuts, seeds, and nut butters, as well as dried fruits, honey, dulse, dried shiitakes, olives, and olive oil.

Lotus Foods, Inc.

921 Richmond Street
El Cerrito, CA 94530
866-972-6879
www.lotusfoods.com

Lotus Foods is doing an amazing job of bringing wonderful, exotic heirloom varieties of rice to Westerners while supporting sustainable agriculture around the world. We have Lotus to thank for Bhutanese red rice, black forbidden rice, Jade Pearl rice, and Madagascar pink rice. They also offer other intriguing varieties of rice, as well as stainless steel rice cookers.

Maine Coast Sea Vegetables

3 Georges Pond Road
Franklin, ME 04634
207-565-2907
www.seaveg.com/shop

This is a one-stop shop for all of your sea vegetable needs: dulse, smoked dulse, digitata (kombu), kelp, laver (wild nori), and more, as well as sea vegetable snacks and seasonings. Their website also offers lots of great sea vegetable recipes.

Maine Seaweed Company

P.O. Box 57
Steuben, ME 04680
207-546-2875
www.alcasoft.com/seaweed

This small, family-owned business offers hand-harvested sea vegetables, including dulse, kelp, laver (wild nori), and digitata (kelp). They also sell seaweed for use as a fertilizer.

Navitas Naturals

9 Pamaron Way, Suite J
Novato, CA 94949
888-645-4282
www.navitasnaturals.com

This is a great source for cacao powder, cacao nibs, goji berries, maca powder, coconut oil, hempseeds, and more.

Nutiva

P.O. Box 1716
Sebastopol, CA 95473
800-993-4367
www.nutiva.com

Nutiva is a good source for hempseeds, hempseed oil, and coconut oil.

She Sells Seaweed

Kacie Loparto
207-546-6449
www.shesellsseaweed.com

Kacie offers dulse, kelp, kombu, wakame, nori, and a soup mix.

Selina Naturally

Four Celtic Drive
Arden, NC 28704
800-867-7258
www.celticseasalt.com

Celtic, Hawaiian, Portugese Sea Salts.

Shiloh Farms

191 Commerce Drive
New Holland, PA 17557
800-362-6832
www.shilohfarms.com

Shiloh Farms offers a wide range of grains, flours, beans, nuts, seeds, sea salts, dried fruits (including goji berries), and healthy sweeteners such as maple sugar and date sugar.

South River Miso Company

888 Shelburne Falls Road
Conway, MA 01341
413-369-4057
www.southrivermiso.com

South River uses time-honored traditional methods to make some of the most intriguing varieties of miso currently available. In addition to typical mellow and aged misos made from brown rice, millet, chickpeas, and adzuki beans, they also offer dandelion leek, garlic red pepper, and sweet white miso.

The Teff Company

P.O. Box A
Caldwell, ID 83606
888-822-2221
www.teffco.com

Who would have thought Ethiopia and Idaho have much in common? As it turns out, Idaho's Snake River Plain offers cropland similar to that where teff is grown in Ethiopia. If you can't find teff at local stores, you can buy both brown and ivory whole teff and their flours online from the Teff Company.

local and organic foods

Farmer's Markets

To find a farmer's market in your area, check the following links:

- Local Harvest's CSA web page: www.localharvest.org/csa

- The U.S. Department of Agriculture's Farmers Markets web page: www.ams.usda.gov/AMSv1.0/farmersmarkets

Community Supported Agriculture

Here are a few resources that can help you find a CSA in your area:

- The Biodynamic Farming and Gardening Association's CSA web page: www.biodynamics.com/csa.html

- The Eat Well Guide: www.eatwellguide.org

- Local Harvest's CSA web page: www.localharvest.org/csa

- Rodale Institute's Farm Locator: www.rodaleinstitute.org/ farm _ locator

- The U.S. Department of Agriculture's CSA web page: www.nal.usda.gov/afsic/pubs/csa/csa.shtml

The Organic Center

www.organic-center.org

The Organic Center is a great source of information on the health benefits of organic foods and agriculture, including scientific research on these topics.

Leslie Cerier, "The Organic Gourmet," is a national authority on gluten-free cooking and baking. She cooks and teaches all over the United States and specializes in whole foods and organic cuisine. She is author of several cookbooks, including *Going Wild in the Kitchen*. Cerier is a chef, educator, environmentalist, photographer, and recipe developer, and is sought after by health professionals and private clients for her expertise in local, seasonal, organic cooking for health and vitality. Visit www.lesliecerier.com for more information.

Foreword writer **Kathie Madonna Swift, MS, RD** is a registered dietitian and a licensed nutritionist. She is codirector of Food as Medicine, a professional nutrition training program. A frequent lecturer, teacher, and consultant, Swift is chair of nutrition at Complementary Care, a dietetic practice group representing dieticians in complementary and alternative medicine.

index

and Millet Stew, 90-91; Jade Rice Pilaf with French Lentils and Toasted Walnuts, 72; Red Lentil and Teff Loaf with Red Wine and Porcini Sauce, 77; Tomato-Lentil Stew with Kale, 146

Leslie's Gluten-Free Peach Pie, 191

liquid-to-grain ratios, 27-28

Living Tree Community Foods, 205

loaves: Coconut Curry Lentil Teff Loaf, 90; Kasha Loaf with Walnuts and Sunflower Seeds, 78-79; Millet Veggie Loaf, 123; Red Lentil and Teff Loaf with Red Wine and Porcini Sauce, 77; Teff Loaf with Red Bell Peppers and African Spices, 76

locally grown foods, 4-5, 208

Loparto, Kacie, 196

Lotus Foods, 18-19, 205

M

maca, 199; Blueberry-Corn Pancakes with Maca, 57; Corn and Quinoa Waffles with Maca, 62; Teff Pancakes with Goji Berries and Maca, 56

Madagascar pink rice, 19; Madagascar Pink Rice with Cashews and Scallions, 129; Mocha Coconut Rice Pudding, 195

main courses, 65-97; African-Spiced Teff and Lentil Stew with Collard Greens and Yams, 82; Brown Rice Spirals in Tomato Sauce with Cauliflower, Olives, and Capers, 69; Butternut Squash and Tempeh Stew with Shiitake Mushrooms, 83; Coconut Curry Lentil and Millet Stew, 90-91; Corn Grits with Sautéed Onion, Kale, and Cheddar, 81; Ethiopian Sunshine Stew, 84-85; Garlicky Peanut Soup, 94-95; Jade Rice

Pilaf with French Lentils and Toasted Walnuts, 72; Kasha Loaf with Walnuts and Sunflower Seeds, 78-79; Quick Miso Soup with Nettles and Spicy Thai Noodles, 96-97; Red Lentil and Teff Loaf with Red Wine and Porcini Sauce, 77; Roasted Vegetable and Quinoa Casserole, 70; Savory Stuffed Winter Squash, 72-73; Shiitake and Kale Lasagna with Marinated Dried Tomatoes and ChPvre, 74-75; Soba with Tempeh and Broccoli in Coconut Sauce, 68; South American Quinoa Stew, 92-93; Summer Pasta and Bean Salad, 67; Sweet Potato and Black Bean Chili with Tomatillos, 88-89; Teff Loaf with Red Bell Peppers and African Spices, 76

Maine Coast Sea Vegetables, 206

Maine Seaweed Company, 206

Maple Sugar Cookies, 179

Marinated Dried Tomatoes, 171

meals: art of preparing, 5-10; choosing foods for, 5-6; colors used in, 7-8; cooking grains for, 25-36; shapes used in, 8; textures used in, 9-10

Mediterranean Rice Salad, 132

Mediterranean Two-Bean Salad, 67

Mediterranean White Bean Salad with Pine Nuts and Capers, 135

milk: almond, 40; coconut, 41; nut and seed, 41

millet, 15-16; Aztec Two-Step side dish, 115; Coconut Curry Lentil and Millet Stew, 90-91; cooking time for, 28, 29; liquid-to-grain ratio for, 28; Millet and Sweet Carrots, 123; Millet Apple Raisin Cake, 184; Millet Croquettes, 123; Millet Veggie Loaf, 123

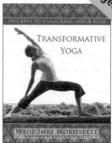

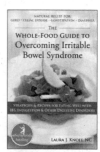